The London-Budapest Game

Sequel to *Sword of the Turul*

Catherine Eva Schandl

The London-Budapest Game
Copyright © 2007 Catherine Eva Schandl
All rights reserved

ISBN 978-1-4303-1178-2
Lulu Books

www.swordoftheturul.com/sequel.html

TABLE OF CONTENTS

INTRODUCTION   6

PART I – HIDDEN WORLDS   7

Chapter 1 – SCOTLAND YARD   9

Chapter 2 – THE PHOTOGRAPH   15

Chapter 3 – THE FIRST BRITISH AGENT   18

Chapter 4 – THE ARRIVAL OF COLONEL HOWIE   22

Chapter 5 – SECRET AGENT ALBERT   28

Chapter 6 – LONDON   36

Chapter 7 – FROM YUGOSLAVIA TO BARI   42

Chapter 8 – ZIONISTS   54

Chapter 9 – THE NEIGHBORHOOD OF RAOUL WALLENBERG   64

Chapter 10 – SECRET NEGOTIATIONS   70

Chapter 11 – CHAOS IN BUDAPEST   79

Chapter 12 – JOEL PALGI'S ESCAPE   86

Chapter 13 – ALLIED ORDERS   88

Chapter 14 – THE SENIOR DUTCH OFFICER   97

Chapter 15 – THE BRITISH MILITARY MISSION   105

Chapter 16 – LIQUIDATION   122

Chapter 17 – TOP SECRET   128

Chapter 18 – THE ENGLISH PATIENT   132

PART II – COLD WAR   135

Chapter 19 – LUBYANKA   136
Chapter 20 – ISOLATION   147
Chapter 21 – THE SWEDES   154
Chapter 22 – FROM POLAND   159
Chapter 23 – THE ADDRESS BOOK   165
Chapter 24 – CANADA/U.S. BORDER   169
Chapter 25 – KINGSMEN OF A CENTURY 172
Chapter 26 – IN HIS WORDS   177
Chapter 27 – SURVEILLANCE   185
Chapter 28 – EPILOGUE   191
PRISON RECORD   196
About Sword of the Turul   197
BIBLIOGRAPHY   199
About the Author   201
INDEX OF NAMES   202

INTRODUCTION

The London-Budapest Game is the sequel to *Sword of the Turul*, offering a unique glimpse into the hidden world of the British underground in World War II Hungary - and its aftermath. Real names are used throughout the book.

From 1991 to 2001, at the request of Raoul Wallenberg's brother, a Swedish-Russian joint Commission was set up to investigate the fate of Swedish Diplomat Raoul Wallenberg. The commission discovered that 3 Hungarian numbered prisoners secretly held in isolation in Vladimir prison, Soviet Union had been connected to the Wallenberg case. One of the three Hungarian numbered prisoners was Karoly Schandl, an idealistic young lawyer in Budapest who had been living near the Swedish Embassy on Gellert Hill. This book is the continuation of his true story. Shocking new information is revealed, supported by historical documents, as well as excerpts from Schandl's private writings.

The anti-Nazi resistance group Karoly Schandl operated in was led by his friend, Gabor Haraszty (Haraszti), a young Hungarian lawyer of Jewish origin. Gabor was known as British intelligence agent ALBERT. The group had links to MI9; British intelligence; Colonel Howie; the Dutch and Polish Underground; the Tito partisans; and a group of famous Jewish parachutists from Palestine, with whom they had planned to collaborate in Hungary.

In an ironic twist of fate, parachutist Joel Palgi once found himself mistaken by the Nazis for the British agent ALBERT.

It was a dangerous game – and only a few would survive ...

Catherine E. Schandl, M.Ed.
July 2007

PART I
HIDDEN WORLDS

"The Highest Council of the Union of Soviet Socialistic Republics has forgiven the crimes for which you were convicted, and you received amnesty ... I have to warn you that whatever you have seen or experienced during the process, in the jails, prison camps, during your imprisonment is a secret of the State. The breach of this secret is an indictable offense against the Soviet State. In effect, it is considered spying. So keep your silence."

CHAPTER 1
SCOTLAND YARD

London, England – mid-1970s

Scotland Yard was having him followed. Right in the middle of an American fast-food outlet in the heart of London, near Piccadilly Circus. A plainclothesman had sat down at their table. Of course, the tail had waited for him to go to the counter to stand in line before approaching his wife and children – but Karoly had seen the entire episode, unfolding before his eyes like some sort of bad dream.

He wondered what their angle was this time. Were they worried he would march over to Whitehall again and demand to speak to someone, as he'd done two decades earlier? It wasn't the first time someone in the group had been hounded by the Yard.

He watched the tall man in the tweed jacket meticulously eat his hamburger in the seat next to his wife, as if it were the most natural thing to do. He then folded the paper it had been wrapped in, and said something to Karoly's wife. The kids were listening intently. Karoly considered yelling at him where he should go, but thought better of it. There must have been another one, lurking quietly in the crowded restaurant. No telling how that one would react.

When the food was finally ready and the overworked girl placed it on his tray with his change, he nodded and proceeded back to the table. Almost on cue, the tail who had been seated with his family stood up and walked out the door. The other one must have given him a signal that Karoly was approaching.

He arrived at the table with the food and tried to force

a smile on his face. His wife and kids were speaking in excited tones about how a man from Scotland Yard had sat at their table.

"I never met anyone from Scotland Yard before!" the youngest exclaimed.

Karoly placed the food on the table and suggested they finish quickly. No one noticed his subdued demeanor because of the slight smile on his face. It proved effective anytime he had to conceal something, as did his unassuming appearance. No one knew it had been cultivated. Conservative clothes, a steady walk, and as often as he could muster, a pleasant, albeit harmless expression.

"What did he say about the Yard?"

His wife seemed perplexed as she remembered. "Nothing."

Of course he didn't say anything about the Yard. Why would he? He had been on a mission to get a message to him – *we know you are here and we are watching you.* How ironic that years ago, the gesture might have actually been welcomed. As it was, their present attention was not appreciated. Not now that he had a family to consider, with a wife too young to know what he'd been through, and North American offspring who couldn't even imagine why across the world, there were files in which their names had been recorded.

In later years, when Karoly was already gone, that would become even more evident as his descendants would be contacted by government supported historians in foreign lands. They would contact his descendants with the certainty that they had reached Karoly's children - because they had seen their names in his file. A file that was halfway across the world. A file that was kept on a man who had been active in the anti-Nazi resistance in World War II Hungary, and who had been working for British intelligence.

Karoly didn't ask his family any more about the man from the Yard.

When they had finally finished their food, he stood up and announced he would meet them back at the flat on St. George Street, as he had an errand to run. They didn't seem to mind, as they'd planned on visiting the famous Harrods department store.

After they said their goodbyes, he was back out in the misty London summer, walking toward a familiar, fashionable street.

He needed answers.

His contact's flat was both Spartan and immaculate, his manners impeccable. Karoly had always admired how "M" had mastered the art of blending in. He wondered at what point the anglophile had become an Englishman. Despite the fact that it was the dead of summer, he was wearing a long-sleeve shirt. As always, it was white.

"I would offer you tea if it weren't for the heat wave. How would you feel about apple cider?"

"Yes, that is fine." Karoly sat in an expensive, uncomfortable armchair and waited for him to return with the glasses.

"It is all natural, you know. Nothing artificial."

"Yes."

"I was not expecting to see you today. It is an impromptu visit."

Karoly leaned forward in the chair and spoke in a low voice. "I was followed. They put a tail on me."

"The KGB?"

"No."

"The Hungarians?"

"No. Scotland Yard." Pause. "I thought the entire matter was over, I thought it ended over a decade ago when they discovered the double agent and his pals."

"You mean the whole ring, I take it. You assumed after they discovered there'd been a ring of Soviet agents, that was that."

"Yes. Everything must have happened because of one

of them."

His contact, "M", paused.

"Are you certain it was Scotland Yard who had you followed today?"

"That was how he introduced himself to my wife and the kids." He went on to describe how the tail had quietly exited moments before he'd returned to the table.

"And you had no contact with anyone here who …"

"You are my only contact here in London from the old days," he stated simply. "The only one who knew me well enough back in Hungary, that is."

"There is always Edward. He is here as well."

"Yes," Karoly agreed, placing his glass on the table. "But he is too much of a celebrity now to want to remember anything about the past."

"M" didn't disagree. "Have you seen him on this visit?"

He shook his head. "No, but we will be dropping by his ex-wife's home tomorrow. She and the Baron have invited us for dinner at their flat."

"Give them my best."

"I will."

"We attended the opera together last month. It was a good performance."

Karoly said nothing. He had never been one for petty conversations, and somehow, that was where things always went with his contact. He cut an impressive image with his anglophile mannerisms, educated English, and military stance – but the talk somehow came back to the mundane. He wondered if it was an attempt to divert his attention.

"M" forced a slight smile, the way he did whenever he wished to present an aura of benevolence. "I shouldn't worry about the Yard. You are here, after all, on a family vacation. Unless, you had intended to meet with …"

"There is no one to meet," he interrupted. "There was no one in Whitehall who wanted to listen to me in late 1956 and early 1957. There is certainly no one there who would like to listen now." He remembered how nervously they had reacted when he marched into Whitehall and asked to speak to someone. He had information, he'd explained. Information about the men from different countries who were secretly held in Soviet prisons.

It wasn't every day that someone who had spent over 11 years secretly held in the Lubyanka, Lefortovo, and Vladimir prisons had such information to share with the British government. But they'd turned him away. They had refused to let him see anyone and they had refused to help a member of his group whom he was sure had still been imprisoned at the time. An Officer of the RAF.

"Perhaps it is just a formality or they are worried you are here to do research."

Karoly was surprised. "Research?"

"For a book on what happened. Perhaps they noticed you've been spending time writing at the British Museum. Perhaps someone reported seeing you there every day."

"You are right about the book."

"M" cleared his throat. "Then you are writing a book? I thought you said you were editing."

"And so I am."

"I assumed you were editing a paper."

"It is actually a professional book. A book on the theory of auditing."

"An academic publication."

He nodded.

His contact appeared relieved. "Then you do not intend to write about what really happened?"

"No." But Karoly did not add that he had in fact already written a paper on his experiences, and it was in the possession of certain organizations, nor did he mention he had several pages of other writings. These were personal matters and he sensed they would make "M" uneasy. Though he possessed a great power of observation and keen intellect, his contact had never given the impression of a man prepared to face any sort of situation head on. That had been Gabor's style. Gabor, the leader of their group, specially trained as an agent of the Secret Intelligence Service, had been a man of action, one not afraid to stand out. And yet he had been betrayed – they all had ...

CHAPTER 2
THE PHOTOGRAPH

Budapest, Hungary
Early 1940s

Karoly Schandl Senior was a lifetime Member of the Hungarian Upper House. He had been appointed a member, in spite of the fact that he was not an aristocrat.

The son of a small landowner, his ability and dedication became evident early on. In 1907, he obtained his doctorate in law (Doctor of Jurisprudence) from the university in Budapest. He was the chairman and organizer/founder of numerous associations, including the nationally well known "Szechenyi Circle," a prestigious association of progressive, liberal thinkers.

By 1921, he had been appointed State Secretary of Agriculture by Prime Minister Count Bethlen. It was a position he kept during the depression years, until 1928, at which time he accepted a post as President of Hangya, the National Production, Trade and Consumer Cooperative.

His entrepreneurial skill and patriotism led Hangya to great success in international trade and profits. A large economic organization, it was a nationwide network of village cooperatives which enabled the farmers to sell their products. Schandl was also an advocate of land reform, in support of small land owners and farmers. Hungary needed change – and he was not afraid to voice his opinion in the Parliament, where he made numerous speeches.

He and his wife Terezia were also active in the FALU movement, which came into existence to improve the economy and circumstances of Hungarian villages.

His Excellency Dr. Karoly Schandl was beloved by his constituents in Devecser, who considered him a patron of the town. Some of them displayed his photograph in prominent places of their family homes.

He had three brothers. One had passed away during the First World War. Another had become a priest and taught at a Piarist School. Karoly Schandl's third brother was Joseph (Jozsef) Schandl, a veterinarian and genetic engineer. *Joseph would later become a renowned, award winning scientist.*

Karoly Schandl had met heads of state worldwide. Officers of the Rockefeller Foundation knew of his work. A devout Catholic, he supported a number of charities, as did his wife Terezia. The family lived in a villa on Gellert Hill, at 16-18 Kelenhegyi Street, across from the Swedish Embassy and next door to the Finnish Embassy, in the Buda part of the city.

The Schandls were pro-British and anti-fascist. The current political landscape in Hungary displeased Mr. Schandl. Behind closed doors, he tried to convince his peers to think of the future, but not all seemed to be listening.

Mr. Schandl's thoughts were solemn when he arrived to have his official photograph taken as a Member of the Upper House.

The appointed photographer asked him to stand behind a well polished table.

He complied.

His dark eyes were piercing as his picture was taken. The appointed photographer was Mr. Veres, the top society photographer of Budapest. His studio was at Gerbeaud Palace, which was where the photographs would be developed.

Like His Excellency Dr. Schandl, he too had a son who would play a key role in the anti-Nazi movement, for he was the father of Thomas Veres.

And Thomas Veres was to become the personal photographer of Swedish diplomat Raoul Wallenberg in the autumn of 1944. He would take the photographs that documented the Holocaust in Budapest – and also put a face to the world's most famous Swedish diplomat.

In the early 1940s in an elegant corner of Budapest, however, neither Mr. Schandl nor Mr. Veres could have foreseen what was to come.

Notes:

The photograph described in this chapter can be seen at

www.karolyschandl.com

CHAPTER 3
THE FIRST BRITISH AGENT

Budapest 1943

In April 1943, Regent Miklos Horthy, the Hungarian head of state, visited Hitler. *Horthy would later report they had not agreed on certain matters – but that did not change the fact that Hungary was still allied with Nazi Germany in the war.*

Horthy then returned to Hungary, to his residence at the Royal Palace, where he lived.

The Budapest Royal Palace had originally been built in the 13th century. It was next to the Castle Hill district and overlooked the city across the Danube River. Castle Hill was an area of Medieval architecture, cobblestone roads, and caves and tunnels unseen beneath the surface.

Clandestine

Among the residences in the Palace was a private apartment belonging to Countess Marie Pejacsevich, a Croatian citizen. The Pejacseviches were an extremely wealthy and eminent aristocratic family of Hungary, the current generation having been born during the era of the Hapsburg dual monarchy.

At the end of May, 1943, Marie's brother, Count Peter Pejacsevich, arrived for a visit from Lisbon to spend time with family. He served as the Croatian envoy in Lisbon and also the authorized Ambassador to Madrid.

Traveling with the Count to Budapest was a medium sized yellow case which he did not speak about to anyone. Upon his arrival at his sister's Palace apartment, he placed it in his private room. Unbeknownst to anyone else, the yellow case contained a short-wave transmitter.

A few weeks passed and the Count was unexpectedly called to Madrid on an urgent matter. Thus, he had no other choice but to leave the secret device and inform his sister of what had been pre-arranged. A British operative was supposed to have already picked up the transmitter. The agent must have been delayed.

The Countess agreed to give the device to the young man on her brother's behalf.

The Count was relieved. He left for Madrid the next day.

Time passed, but still no one came for the secret yellow case. After a number of weeks, the Countess herself had to leave Budapest on family business for two weeks. What was she to do – inform someone else of the transmitter? She decided not to, as the current situation in Budapest made it far too risky. Such a secret device could undoubtedly lead to the arrest of anyone connected to it, for it was, after all, a radio of the Allies. And so, the Countess took her leave without telling anyone about the secret case and its contents …

One day in August, her brother Count Geza Pejacsevich, received an unexpected visitor at his sister's Palace apartment.

The young Hungarian man nodded and then said the secret code.

"Peter Madrid."

Count Geza was perplexed.

The young man explained. "The transmitter. I am here to collect it." Geza replied that unfortunately, he did not have any information about a transmitter.

The young man looked at him for a long time and asked whether the Countess was present.

"Not at the moment. She has gone to the country."

The young man quietly departed, declining to leave his

name.

Eventually, the Countess returned home from her trip and her brother informed her of the unusual visitor. She became worried. What if the individual had really been an agent provocateur? She consulted her third brother, Count Marcus Pejacsevich, about the incident. Together they came up with a plan. The two brothers would leave Budapest, travel to another location, and bury the radio there, to be on the safe side. They did precisely that.

In order to remove all traces of the device, the Countess herself burned the key to the case and all of the cipher papers.

In September, the same young man showed up at the apartment again. He asked to speak with the Countess, who was present and received him.

He apologized for the two month delay and added that in this kind of work, one had to expect such delays. For matters of security, he did not inform her that he'd been parachuted into Poland the previous March and had made his way to Budapest on sheer skill and courage. The British had set it all up. He was the very first agent they dispatched into Hungary - via an airdrop into Poland - and he was to pick up the radio. The one that the ambassador in Madrid had brought by train.

The Countess said she understood about the delay and then said that the transmitter had been buried elsewhere.

"Do you recall the exact location?"

She told him she did, and passed on the information to him.

The young man thanked her, told her not to worry, and then disappeared. They never saw him again, never learned his real identity.

His name was Clement - and he would later prove to be one of the most active agents of the Secret Intelligence Service in World War II Hungary …

Notes:

Based on information from

1. HS 4/129
   The Clement/Vajda Report (translated from German)

2. W. Mackenzie, *The Secret History of S.O.E.* (St. Ermin's Press 2000, 2002)

3. HS 4/103

CHAPTER 4
THE ARRIVAL OF COLONEL HOWIE

In 1943, an imposing South African artillery colonel arrived in Hungary, having escaped from a POW camp. His experiences read like an adventure story. Having been captured at Tobruk, he became a prisoner in Italy. In August 1943, he had been moved to Stalag 8B at Breslau. Upon his arrival at the camp, he got in touch with the Escape Committee and was soon able to make his escape by crawling through a tunnel. He was Lieutenant-Colonel Charles Telfer Howie.[1]

Howie had been assisted and accompanied by a resourceful young man known as "Tom." In reality, "Tom" was a Hungarian-born Jewish Palestinian in British uniform. His name was Weinstein and he was one of the first Jewish Hungarians from Palestine to re-enter Hungary as a British soldier.[2]

Colonel Howie's original plan had been to join the Tito partisans in Yugoslavia. He and Weinstein eventually reached Hungary through Silesia. As he was unable to establish a link to the Tito partisans right away, he remained in Hungary and became involved with the Polish and Dutch Underground. He spoke English, Afrikaans, and while a prisoner, had learned to read French, German, and Italian, though he could not speak or read Hungarian.[3]

As he was South African, he also spoke some Dutch, which had enabled him to pass himself off as a Dutch engineer while en route to Budapest.[4]

Howie ended up at the Polish internment camp in Zugliget, on the outskirts of Budapest, on the Buda side of the capital. He made contact with a number of influential people at Zugliget. Among his confidants were the Polish Countess Tarnopolska and other aristocrats. The countess soon put him in touch with a young Dutch Officer by the name of Gerit Van der Waals. Van der Waals was extremely active in the Underground, having been the first Dutch Officer in Hungary. He was periodically used as a courier ("cut-out") by the British and had a number of contacts among the Dutch, as well as the Poles. At Howie's request, he introduced the South African Colonel to Smit, Director of Philips radio in the Balkans. Smit then transmitted for Howie details of his situation, along with other information, to Ankara. Through Smit, Howie managed to communicate with the British attaché in Ankara. [5]

Through a Hungarian countess, Howie also made the acquaintance of Prince Andrew Sapieha, the Hungarian representative of General Bor, head of the AK - the Polish Home Army. In a short period of time, his contacts were numerous. [6]

Though industrious and capable a soldier, Howie lacked any intelligence training and there were reports of complaints by the Hungarians concerning his lack of security as early as 1943. [7] Howie admittedly was not particularly fond of Hungarians, but spoke highly of the Reverend Szent-Ivanyi, at whose church hostel he ended up hiding for a year following his stay in Zugliget. [8]

At Howie's request, the secret Polish Underground Organization helped him set up a small W/T station at the reverend's house. It worked every two days. Most of the traffic he received was from Warsaw, though any messages to Poland had to be taken over land from Budapest to Warsaw. The Polish Underground regularly arranged for various supplies to reach Poland from Hungary, including radio equipment from Smit's factory. Howie was also able to maintain contact with London with the W/T, though his lack of a code proved to be rather inconvenient. [9]

Colonel Howie was put in charge of the Allied prisoners of war, who were still protected by the Hungarian government. He soon appointed a New Zealander, Captain

Roy Natusch, to oversee the Englishers who were interned in the Szigetvar Castle of Count Andrassy, in the southern part of the country. Howie, however, chose to remain in the capital. [10]

Telfer, as the Reverend Szent-Ivanyi called him, had not originally come to Hungary in the capacity of a secret agent, as some suspected. He was simply the highest ranking British Officer in Hungary at the time.

Weinstein, Howie, and Joel Brand

Weinstein, who had returned to his country of birth along with the Colonel, was required to follow Howie's orders, as he himself was a British soldier in Hungary. So when the British Colonel later asked him to introduce him to Zionist Joel Brand, Weinstein telephoned Brand to arrange a meeting. [11]

Brand agreed. He played a key role in the Jewish Aid and Rescue Committee, a group of Zionists in Budapest whose function was to help Jews escape. A difficult task indeed. Himself a Jewish Hungarian-born European, Brand was a courageous man to remain in the inferno of mass deportations and the inevitable death and destruction that would await when the Germans arrived – a scenario many believed was imminent.

Weinstein, Brand, and Howie met near the church where Howie had been hiding. The Colonel asked Sergeant Weinstein to leave him alone with Brand. [12]

Howie then reportedly attempted to enlist Brand's commitment to help organize acts of sabotage behind enemy lines as well as armed resistance – yet it was his second request that led to the strongest disagreement.[13]

The Colonel informed Brand that he would like to use the fifty certificates per month Brand received from England for providing Jewish Hungarian children safe passage to Palestine. Howie was of the opinion that they should be used for Allied soldiers instead – specifically, English military personnel. He then reportedly demanded the certificates be available to English and Allied Officers, pilots, technicians, etc. [14]

Brand refused. His organization was in the business of saving the lives of as many Jewish citizens as possible. Besides, as he later pointed out, he was already helping in false documents as well as other ways. [15]

This led to a strong disagreement. Howie became angry. Still, Brand refused to give him the certificates that had been intended for Jewish children. [16]

The meeting did not have the outcome the British Colonel desired. But Howie, now commonly referred to as the leader of the Allied POWs in Hungary, would not give up on his goal of organizing armed resistance ...

Howie's Role

In February 1944, the London Special Operations Executive (SOE) received word that Howie would be willing to work for them in Hungary. As it turned out, he had already been in communication with the British A-Force for three months. The A-Force was a Cairo-based organization whose role was deception and escape. They had sent Colonel Howie instructions on how to proceed to Yugoslavia. Yet he had opted to remain in Hungary, where he believed he could be of better use to the A-Force. The A-Force agreed to his proposal and sent him instructions and details concerning their agents, in addition to arranging for him to receive a certain sum. Howie was to become a center of the A-Force escape organization in Hungary. However, due to his circumstances and the fact that he was not considered as guarded as a real secret operative would have been, Howie's duties, according to the A-Force, were best kept at an information level, rather than active involvement. Such was the message relayed to the SOE (Special Operations Executive) by the A-Force on February 10, 1944. [17]

Things were about to change drastically in the capital. In March 1944, Hitler summoned Regent Admiral Nicholas Horthy and his cabinet to a meeting. They were informed that as Hungary was no longer considered a trustworthy ally, Germany was going to occupy the country. The inevitable was about to become a reality. Days later, on March 19, 1944, the Germans marched into Hungary. During the German occupation, Sztojay, the former Hungarian Minister in Berlin, established a new government, though the SS and Reich Plenipotentiary Edmund Vessenmayer controlled the reigns of power. Miklos Kallay, who had been the Prime Minister since 1942 - and had refused to deport Jewish Hungarians to Poland - went into hiding in the Turkish Embassy.[18]

The Gestapo captured most of the prisoners at Szigetvar and deported them to Germany. The remaining few dispersed and went into hiding. There were Nazis everywhere.[19]

Adolf Eichmann had arrived in Budapest. He was about to take charge of "Jewish matters." [20]

Needless to say, Howie's position became extremely precarious following the German invasion of March 19, 1944. He hastily disassembled his wireless set, distributing the parts, and went more deeply under cover. He lost contact with a number of his usual Allies, who had since dispersed, and then attempted to regroup ... [21]

Notes:

1. HS 9/753/2 *(SOE Personnel File of Howie)*
2. K. Kapronczay, *Refugees in Hungary: Shelter from the Storm During World War II* (Matthias Corvinus Publishing 1999)
3. HS 9/753/2 *(SOE Personnel File of Howie)*
4. K. Kapronczay, *Refugees in Hungary: Shelter from the Storm During World War II* (Matthias Corvinus Publishing 1999)
5. HS 9/753/2 *(SOE Personnel File of Howie)*
6. Ibid
7. Ibid
8. Ibid
9. Ibid
10. K. Kapronczay *Refugees in Hungary: Shelter from the Storm During World War II* (Matthias Corvinus Publishing 1999)
11. Alex Weissberg, *Desperate Mission: Joel Brand's Story* (Criterion Books 1958)
12. Alex Weissberg, *Desperate Mission: Joel Brand's Story* (Criterion Books 1958)
13. Joel Brand's Testimony, *Eichmann Trial Transcripts*, (Nizkor Project)
14. Ibid
15. Ibid
16. Ibid
17. HS 9/753/2 *(SOE Personnel File of Howie)*
18. U.S. National Archives State Dept. and Foreign Affairs Records, *Records of the Foreign Service Posts of the Dept. of State (RG84)*
19. K. Kapronczay *Refugees in Hungary: Shelter from the Storm During World War II* (Matthias Corvinus Publishing 1999)
20. *Eichmann Trial Transcripts*, (Nizkor Project)
21. HS 9/753/2 *(SOE Personnel File of Howie)*

CHAPTER 5
SECRET AGENT ALBERT

The Secret History of the Special Operations Executive (SOE), which was quietly prepared for the British Cabinet in 1945, includes not only some of the better known groups that had approached the Allies with proposals for peace and government, but also the general British overview of the Hungarian situation. [1]

The original base of the Hungarian section of SOE had been in Istanbul. By late 1942, there had been a reported increase in feelers put out from Hungary's official circles to the British. According to the secret report, Professor Szent-Gyorgyi, a renowned Hungarian scientist, appeared in Istanbul and presented a plan for a new government. It was a plan for an anti-Nazi coalition government in which he should be the Prime Minister. Also worthy of mention were the activities of Tibor Eckhardt and the "Free Hungarians" in the U.S., as well as the activities of the Archduke Otto. Unfortunately, the fact that there was more than one group admittedly caused some confusion for the British, including the SOE - which Churchill had created to *set Europe ablaze.* [2]

Their interest lay more in armed resistance than politics, though they did have pro-British contacts to help along with clandestine missions in diplomatic circles, such as Count Peter Pejacsevich in Madrid.

In 1943, when Laszlo Veres - whom the British regarded as a minor Hungarian official - ventured to Istanbul to offer the surrender of Hungary on behalf of a powerful group in Prime Minister Kallay's government, the SOE was listening. However, they were not experienced or adept in matters of a diplomatic nature. The Hungarians sought a guarantee that they would be spared of communism and that the Anglo-Americans would arrive in Hungary before the Russians. What they had perhaps not realized was that in 1940, a British Colonel (Guiness) had signed an agreement - on behalf of the British Commonwealth - with the NKVD in Moscow. It was an agreement which involved, among other things, cooperation and liaison missions between the SOE and the NKVD. [3]

The SOE agreed to place a wireless set in the Hungarian Foreign Office and pressured the Hungarians to agree to an Allied mission to Hungary – a military one. The SOE would send in the mission so as to organize and assist the Hungarians in resistance activities against the Germans. The Hungarians agreed but the British Foreign Office hesitated, not wanting to irk Moscow by sending a British military mission into an anti-communist Axis country. [4]

By March 1944, when they finally did agree, it was already too late. The mission never materialized. The Germans marched into Hungary on March 19. Prime Minister Kallay went into hiding at the Turkish Embassy. Veres and others fled the country.

By then, Karoly Schandl and Gabor Haraszty, both of whom lived relatively close to Zugliget, had been actively involved for quite some time in the highly secretive world of the British-led underground in Budapest. They had been recruited by an old Polish friend. [5]

In 1939, "Jack" escaped from Poland to Hungary. Karoly and his close friends the Haraszty brothers (Gabor and Karoly Haraszty) had made his acquaintance at a Boy Scouts Jamboree in 1932 Poland. When Jack fled to Hungary from Poland, in need of food and shelter, the old friends from the Piarist Boy Scouts group came to his aide. They fed him, and sheltered him. [6]

Jack was in regular contact with the Polish Legation and after it had left Budapest, remained in the capital as an agent. He was with the Inter-Service Liaison Department (ISLD/MI6) and one by one, he recruited his old friends from that group to help the cause. They were enthusiastic, capable, and committed to the cause of helping both Jewish Hungarians and Polish citizens.[7] They were also from wealthy and influential families who opposed the Nazis and Arrow Cross fascists.

The Arrow Cross had gained 20 percent of the seats in the government prior to the war. Everyone knew what their mandate really was – and it was one of hatred and intolerance.

It was a dangerous time to be involved in the underground. Karoly and Gabor were both lawyers. Karoly had two offices – one at the OKH (*Országos Központi Hitelszövetkezet*), which was connected to Hangya. The second office was in his upstairs private apartment in the family villa at 16-18 Kelenhegyi Street. There were other useful spaces in his apartment – namely a secret closet, and a darkroom for developing photographs. He was still able to go on with the pretense of everyday living, yet Gabor's situation was different. He was of Jewish origin and the Nazis considered him a Jew.[8]

Despite the risks, he was not going to sit back and let the Nazis win; he was ready for action. Gabor and Karoly were actively involved in helping escaped Allied prisoners of war reach the Allies via Yugoslavia and the Tito partisans. In addition, the group was gathering intelligence which was then reported to Jack. They served as messengers and couriers as well. Monthly reports to the Center were handed over with the escaped Allies they delivered to the Tito partisans, who then transported the escaped POWs back to Bari with the supply plane. Karoly made many of the deliveries to the Yugoslav border himself, as navigation had always been his forte.[9]

There were other old Piarist school friends assisting the cause. Peter Zerkowitz, descended from a famous Hungarian composer, was later described by the British A-Force as a "helper" for hiding an Allied POW, among his other activities. He was dealing with various groups in the Underground resistance.

Istvan Szent-Miklosy of the Hungarian Independence

Movement referred to the Zerkowitz brothers as members of the resistance with whom his group had had friendly communications.[10] Peter Zerkowitz had also provided Szent Miklosy with false documents.

Szent-Miklosy is described in the British archives as a member of the "Kallay Group." [11]

Other designated "helpers" of the British were Raphael Rupert as well as Charles Szladits, a bank barrister who represented the legal interests of the British Council in Hungary and also American interests in Hungary.[12]

> As Gabor Haraszty would later write in one of his reports for Bari ...
>
> *"One good helper who knows the position of all the prisons and about prisoners is Mr. Charles Szladits of the Commercial Bank, Budapest, he is the barrister of the bank."* [13]

Raphael Rupert, a lawyer and graduate of a Piarist School in Budapest, had some interesting contacts, including someone called "Rainprecht," who provided members of the underground with disguises.[14]

Rupert and Szladits were the administrators of a villa where a number of Allied POWs were successfully hidden.[15] The villa was actually the property of Minister Antal, listed in the British archives as a helper.[16]

Among the hidden downed airmen would be RAF Officer, Reginald Barratt, who had escaped from Szigetvar and ended up working closely with Gabor and his friends in Budapest.

In early 1944, Gabor Haraszty was trained to become an official agent of the British Intelligence Service.

He was then known as ALBERT. [17]

Meanwhile, Colonel Howie was still in Budapest and was in the process of regrouping. He got in touch with the Hungarian Communist Underground movement, but found no one important among them and perceived that they were for the most part inactive and simply waiting for orders. [18]

But there were also others in the capital – and some were already conducting clandestine work against the Nazis. Howie soon allied himself with an extensive network. There were Poles with French code names - who were in fact with the British Intelligence Service - Hungarians of the British Intelligence Service, and the Dutch Officers who worked alongside them. The Dutch side was led by Lieutenant Edward J.C. Van Hootegem of the Royal Dutch Army (Royal Guards Hunters). [19]

Also in the network was Jack, Karoly's and Gabor's Polish friend from the old Boy Scouts jamboree. As Karoly always used to say, one of Jack's aliases in Hungary was Dubreuil. Jacques Dubreuil.

As later reported to the British by Lieutenant Van Hootegem, the successful network had involved meetings including Lt. Van Hootegem, Mr. Dubreuil, Mr. Lafayette, and South African Colonel Howie, all of whom had been working for the Secret Intelligence Service. The group met on several occasions to coordinate activities as well as share intelligence. And the official radio operator was Clement, also a British agent. [20]

Karoly Schandl knew Clement well, as did Gabor Haraszty - which is not surprising. They were all part of the network - and they all reported to Dubreuil (Jack). Clement, the first British agent to be dispatched to Hungary by being dropped into Poland, was, in fact, a Hungarian who could speak fluent Polish.

He had originally been with the Special Operations Executive. [21]

It was this network which successfully liberated from Hungarian camps and prisons a number of English and Allied POWs, some of whom stayed, others who were taken to Bari via the Tito partisans in Yugoslavia. The network also gathered intelligence for the Allies – intelligence concerning airfields, factories, and oil refineries. This military intelligence was then transmitted by means of Clement (Klement), who operated the short wave radio set, and passed on the information to the Secret Intelligence Service.[22]

OCCUPATION

The situation, however, was simply intolerable for Hungary's Jewish citizens, and Gabor Haraszty resolved to do more. Thus, he decided to make a journey to the Allied Headquarters in Bari via the Tito partisans with significant information to help POWs and plan Jewish escape routes. In addition, he was carrying a message on behalf of former Prime Minister Kallay. Gabor prepared to leave Budapest and meet the Allies, including a group of incredible Jewish parachutists.

He left Hungary as ALBERT on May 15, 1944 ... [23]

Meanwhile, Joel Brand of the Jewish Aid and Rescue Committee had been summoned by Eichmann to a meeting at the Majestic Hotel in Budapest. Upon his arrival, he was taken directly to Eichmann's office on the ground floor. Eichmann was wearing his SS uniform. There was also a civilian present. At the time, Brand did not know the identity of the civilian, but would later learn that he was SS Lieutenant Kurt Becher.[24]

Eichmann bellowed at Brand that he was in charge of the "Action" operation and it was now Hungary's turn. He said he wanted to make a deal – goods for blood. He proposed to sell one million Jews in exchange for goods. He later clarified his demand – he would release one million Jews for 10,000 new trucks that were winter operational. The trucks were to be used on the Eastern Front.[25]

Eichmann stated that once the Allies had agreed to his proposal and he received such confirmation, he would release the first 100,000 Jews. He also promised to blow up the murderous gas chambers at Auschwitz. [26]

Brand prepared to take this message to Istanbul and consult with the Jewish Agency. [27]

He left Hungary on May 16, 1944 – one day after Gabor Haraszty left for Bari ... [28]

Notes:

1. W. Mackenzie, *The Secret History of S.O.E.* (St. Ermin's Press 2000, 2002)
2. Ibid
3. Ibid
4. Ibid
5. C. Schandl, *Sword of the Turul* (Lulu Press 2005)
6. Ibid
7. Ibid
8. Ibid
9. Ibid
10. Istvan Szent-Miklosy, *With the Hungarian Independence Movement 1943-1947* (Praeger Publishers 1988)
11. HS 4/129
12. Ibid
13. WO 208/3381 (see Albert's report)
14. HS 4/129
15. Stephen Kertesz, *Between Russia and the West* (University of Notre Dame Press 1984)
16. HS 4/129
17. C. Schandl, *Sword of the Turul* (Lulu Press 2005)
18. HS 9/753/2 *(SOE Personnel File of Howie)*
19. HS 4/103
20. Ibid
21. W. Mackenzie, *The Secret History of S.O.E.* (St. Ermin's Press 2000, 2002) *see "Klement."*
22. HS 4/103
23. WO 208/3381 (see Albert's report)
24. Joel Brand's Testimony, *Eichmann Trial Transcripts*, (Nizkor Project)
25. Ibid
26. Ibid
27. Ibid
28. Alex Weissberg, *Desperate Mission: Joel Brand's Story* (Criterion Books 1958)

CHAPTER 6
LONDON

London, England
mid-1970s

    Karoly Schandl left his contact's flat and proceeded to walk through the dreary grayness of London. As always, his footsteps were quick and purposeful. He had never been a man to waste energy – or words. His interest had always been in facts, not the foolish niceties of the mundane. Still, there was something which continued to draw him to the world of the English, in spite of all that had occurred. He ignored the raindrops which had started to fall and wondered if it was simply a piece of his lost youth which made him feel at home here, though he could never bring himself to stay indefinitely. His lost youth. In the 1930s, he'd spent a year at Cambridge University as a post-graduate research student. He had attended the Wednesday seminars of John Maynard Keynes.

    Cambridge – the university where Kim Philby had started his illustrious Soviet spy career. Karoly used to talk about the ironies of his life, and among them was always included that, unbeknownst to him, Kim Philby and his associates had already infiltrated the Cambridge student body by the time Karoly had arrived. It was just one of those ironies of his life. Another irony was how he'd ended up imprisoned in the Soviet Union for over 11 years, including 5 years in Vladimir Prison, where the Soviets had isolated famous prisoners and Generals. He did not consider himself famous and he was certainly not a General.

    He paused at a crosswalk and waited for the lights to change. A double-decker bus rolled past. His visit to his old contact had done him a world of good. His contact was one who believed in putting the past in the past and leaving it there. This was evident in his speech and mannerisms. He had almost perfected his image as an Englishman.

The light finally changed and Karoly walked across the narrow street alongside the other pedestrians, none of whom seemed to take any notice of him. His contact may have become almost English, but Karoly had mastered the art of being almost invisible. He'd had to in order to survive. The secret meetings and deliveries in the midst of Nazi occupied terrain, the refugees whose lives had been depending on him, his subsequent arrest, the interrogations – they had all shaped who he was.

And then there was Whitehall. When he'd finally made it to the free world in '56, it had been one of his first destinations. In his idealism, he'd actually assumed they would wish to know all the facts and take action. After all, it wasn't every day that a man could tell them of how the NKVD had liquidated a group of British agents and how a Royal Air Force pilot who had been helping them was still in Soviet captivity. Yet they had, by all appearances, not wanted to hear about it, as they had not allowed him to speak to anyone of importance. To make matters worse, they acted as though they were afraid of him. And he had gone there more than once. In December 1956, he had ventured to Whitehall several times, but no one, it seemed, wanted to know about the RAF Officer who was still imprisoned in the Soviet Union. "He was one of theirs!" he used to exclaim whenever bringing up the matter. "One of their own!" [1]

Karoly had found himself otherwise welcomed by the British. After his arrival in 1956, he had found work almost immediately as an interpreter at the Coal Board. In Newcastle, the Rotary Club had invited him to speak of his experiences in Soviet prisons and the talk had been reported in the Evening Sentinel newspaper. Yet still, there was Whitehall. The knowledge that they would do nothing was intolerable. In the end, he had turned down the position he was offered as a researcher, and left for North America. [2]

It was a world away from the past, though no one is ever truly free of the past. Perhaps that was what had prompted him to make the last minute reservation to London and whisk his family to the city for a month. Perhaps he had been drawn to his past. The moment he set foot on British soil, the group suddenly became a reality again. In North America, it seemed little more than a faraway memory of a world long past.

But they had been real – as real as your breath on a cold London day. Young, handsome, educated, well traveled – and all progressive thinkers. They would have seen to it that Hungary had a bright future. They were the sons of high ranking, internationally respected politicians, famous composers, judges, and other men of influence. A number of them were of Jewish origin and they knew each other from the same organization – the Piarist High School Boy Scouts. And it was that Boy Scout spirit which survived and made the few who knew of their group's existence marvel at their enthusiasm. [3]

There were matters to discuss in meetings, reports to prepare, and information to gather, for both the original group members as well as the contacts they soon made. Each had his own talents, whether hidden or evident. Gabor had been thorough and logical, as had Karoly, while their close contact Clement's inquisitive mind and talent in document forgeries were well put to use in the secret printing press he also helped operate in Budapest.

Courage was a trait they all possessed, for to conduct such clandestine operations under the nose of the Gestapo entailed a continuous risk of arrest, torture, and execution. Ironically, Karoly's home was located just across the bridge from the Gestapo Headquarters. But it did not deter him, nor did it prevent Gabor, Clement, and airman Reginald Barratt from paying regular visits to his apartment. [4]

They came to the house often, disguised as monks with robes supplied by the Cave Church down the street.

It was all part of the game – a game they had no doubt they would win against the Nazis.

He remembered how the British had trained Gabor as an official British agent of the Secret Intelligence Service, to organize and lead the group in early 1944. That was when he'd become known as ALBERT. [5] Clement had been a British agent as well – of the Special Operations Executive.

But that was all in the past.

The London rain became heavier and Karoly continued to ignore it. By the time he had returned to the British Museum, it was late afternoon. He would spend a little time here to collect his thoughts for his text on auditing, and would then return to the flat he'd rented for his family for the month.

The flat was in a newly renovated area on St. George Street. The building had a smart white exterior, though the back view was less elegant, looking onto an unattractive alley where neighbors hung their laundry. Majestic on one side, yet unfinished and sorely lacking on the other. It was only the nice façade which was visible to passersby.

It reminded him of the less than perfect exterior of English society, which was not always visible to an outsider. Nevertheless, even as in the past, all things English appealed to the Budapesters who had once hoped to make their world at least half as functional, for here, one could not deny, there was at least some form of democracy at work.

The British Museum echoed Karoly's pensive silence as he entered. The Reading Room of the museum, as always, did not appear to be full, not due to a lack of people inside, but because the imposing dome roof gave it an aura of emptiness. Cultured emptiness. If one were a serious researcher, one had access to the famous room, where many a notable figure had passed hours reading, researching, and thinking.

He sat down and reminded himself that he was there to put the finishing touches on his scholarly work.

Unbeknownst to Karoly Schandl, at the same time, two historians were also conducting research in the U.K. Their research was on MI9, the Secret British Service that specialized in the escape and evasion of Allied airmen shot down behind enemy lines during the Second World War. They were M.R.D. Foot and J.M. Langley. [6]

Foot, a former Officer, was originally from London and was an experienced history professor and historical researcher. His teaching career included twelve years at Oxford University. His colleague for the book, J.M. Langley, had been active in MI6 during the war, as the head of MI9's department which dealt with Northwest Europe. To his credit was also that he had successfully arranged the safe return of some 3000 people to England. [7]

Foot and Langley had at their disposal a number of classified records to help tell the story of MI9 and many of its heroes and escaped prisoners of war. When they researched Hungary, they came across a report in the British archives which had been written in 1944, by a British agent whom Simonds, the head of MI9, seemed to have placed at the Hungarian/Yugoslav border. According to reports, in the summer of 1944, this agent provided useful information to the Allies in Bari, after taking a month to come through Yugoslavia and the Tito partisans. He also met with some of the Jewish parachutists who had arrived in Yugoslavia.

Foot and Langley were unable to identify him except by his code name. [8]

And as their book reported in an obscure footnote when it was first published in 1979, the unknown agent's code name was ALBERT ... [9]

Notes:

1. C. Schandl, *Sword of the Turul* (Lulu Press 2005)
2. Ibid
3. Ibid
4. HS 9/461/7
5. Schandl, *Sword of the Turul* (Lulu Press 2005)
6. M.R.D. Foot & J.M. Langley, *MI9 Escape and Evasion 1939-1945* (Bodley Head 1979)
7. Ibid
8. Ibid
9. Ibid

CHAPTER 7
FROM YUGOSLAVIA TO BARI

"It is just one month from the time of my leaving Budapest to my arrival in Bari. I had no difficulty in reaching the Yugoslavian border." [1]

Gabor Haraszty, a.k.a. ALBERT
June 1944

May 1944

On May 15, 1944, Gabor Haraszty (ALBERT) left Budapest for southern Hungary, where he intended to cross the Hungarian/Yugoslav border. He carried a false identification document which enabled him to travel to the south by train. [2]

In order to disguise himself, he had dyed his hair and was wearing glasses, of which he had no need. The glasses had clear lenses. [3]

Thus, he did not have the appearance of Gabor Haraszty, the Hungarian lawyer from Budapest, and there was no risk of him being spotted and turned over to the Gestapo.

One had to be extremely cautious, as with the Nazi occupation, there had been an increase in the number of German Secret Service agents – among the Hungarian population. Even Reverend Szent-Ivanyi had remarked that one never knew whether one was speaking to an old friend or a member of the Nazi Secret Service.

A number of good men had already been arrested. Roy Natusch, whom Howie had appointed to oversee the POWs hiding at Count Andrassy's Szigetvar castle, had been taken away by the Gestapo (he later escaped). Count Andrassy and his wife, who had hidden the POWs on their estate, had also been arrested by the Gestapo. Count Andrassy had been a confidant of Colonel Howie concerning the attempt to arrange a certain "Sandy" mission to the Kallay government. The mission was to have been received on his estate. [4]

Colonel Howie had expressed an interest in the possibility of himself venturing to Yugoslavia to join the Tito partisans. He was presently hiding in a flat which was, ironically, not far from Gestapo Headquarters. [5]

Gabor was able to cross the Hungarian/Yugoslav border at Herginitza. From there, he proceeded to Ivanitika, in the Kalnik area. He used his code name – ALBERT. [6]

ALBERT was on an important diplomatic mission. He was carrying secret letters from Prime Minister Kallay, who was still in hiding at the Turkish Embassy in Budapest. The Hungarian Prime Minister had written a communiqué to Churchill, stating that Hungary wished to surrender to the Allied forces.[7] In addition, there was talk of a pro-British rebellion.

ALBERT was the diplomatic messenger. [8]

He was also about to make contact with the Palestinian Jewish parachutists who had been dropped behind enemy lines to assist with resistance and rescue operations. They had been trained by the British and they were all volunteers.

They included:

Hannah Senesh (MINNIE)
Reuven Dafni (GARY)
Perez Goldstein (JONES)
Joel Palgi (MICKY/HULBERT)
Sgt. Berdichev (WILLIS)

When Gabor entered Yugoslavia as ALBERT, he soon met up with Reuven Dafni. [9]

Dafni had been given GARY as his code name on account of the fact that he looked like movie star Gary Cooper – and it was his nickname.[10] He was extremely well liked. He had been born in Zagreb, Yugoslavia, then moved to Austria with his family as a teenager. At the age of 23, Reuven moved to Palestine, where he helped found a Kibbutz. He was drafted into the British Army in 1940 and soon joined a famous unit of Jewish paratroopers whose mission would be to rescue Jews behind enemy lines and help them get to Palestine. [11]

The task at hand was to set up an operational line of evasion. MI9 called it the "Chicken Mission." [12]

Reuven Dafni had been parachuted into Yugoslavia, where his role in the Chicken Operation was to remain there with Major John Eden (the nephew of the British foreign minister), assist agents, and help the Jewish refugees who were to be smuggled out of Hungary, en route to Palestine. Reuven, a natural leader, soon took charge. [13]

Gabor spoke to Reuven and agreed to introduce him to the Frenchman who had helped his traveling group to reach Kalnik. He then spoke with Hannah Senesh (Anna Szenes) at length about the current situation in Hungary.[14]

The courageous Jewish poetess, who had moved from Hungary to Palestine, was part of the Chicken I Operation, whose mission would be to help organize escape routes from Hungary. Hannah's code name was MINNIE.[15] The daughter of a famous Hungarian playwright, she was also from Budapest.

> *"I gave instructions to MINNIE how to go to Budapest. I sent her with a Frenchman to act as guide, this is the Frenchman who brought me through. I have talked to MINNIE on conditions in Hungary for 6 hours one day and 3 hours another." [16]*
>
> *Gabor Haraszty (ALBERT)*

Perez Goldstein, code name JONES, was another member of the Chicken operations. He was asked to confirm ALBERT's identity, so he made contact with his authorities by way of his W/T set. When ALBERT's identity had been confirmed, the mood became hopeful. [17]

With the important message Gabor was carrying on behalf of Kallay for Churchill, there was the possibility of something significant in the air. Unfortunately, nothing would materialize from the delivery - for men and women on the ground in times of war are often unable to change the course of the policy makers. However, no one at that time suspected as much. ALBERT had arrived with news from Budapest, he was carrying an important message to the British, he himself was a British agent, and he was eager to offer all assistance possible to the brave parachutists.

Gabor gave Hannah Senesh the name of useful contacts in Budapest, so as to aid the Chicken I operation. He also provided Reuven Dafni (GARY) with the names of good friends in Budapest who knew "the position," as well as information on how to procure false documents once prisoners had escaped. [18]

He advised them that if one wished to be treated well in Hungary, it was best to pretend to be French, as the Hungarians did not presently permit the Germans to arrest the French. If one could speak French, he explained, one ought to pose as Vichy French, pretending to have entered Hungary for work and/or because one despised the Germans. All French people were well treated in Hungary – even the French prisoners. [19]

A few days later, Gabor left Kalnik for Cazma. Eden soon arrived, in order to meet him and hear of the important message he carried. They spoke at length, though the details of their conversation are not known. [20]

Gabor noted that MICKY had not yet arrived in Cazma and he had missed meeting him. [21] MICKY was the alias of parachutist Joel Palgi, a Jewish Hungarian from Transylvania who'd moved to Palestine as a teenager. A childhood friend of

Perez Goldstein, he too was to play a key role in the operations. [22]

On June 13, 1944, as per a secret cipher message - due to the arrival of an ISLD agent with significant intelligence, it was decided that a Lysander plane should be sent to transport him to Bari, once Istanbul had checked his identity. [23]

On June 14, 1944, Squadron Leader Lawson sent a cipher message to Simonds, informing him that ALBERT (the above mentioned ISLD agent) had now arrived in Bari. Meanwhile, Hannah Senesh was en route to Hungary with a radio. Lawson also stated that he was hoping to interview ALBERT. [24]

Lawson, a British Intelligence Officer and RAF wing commander, was the Jewish liaison between British Intelligence and the Palestinian parachutists. [25]

ALBERT was looking forward to meeting him as well.

BARI

Albert's Report

In his June 15, 1944 report to Lawson, Gabor Haraszty (ALBERT) stated that he had no difficulty in reaching the Yugoslav/Hungarian border. He showed the false identity document he had used to travel by train in Hungary. [26]

He also brought up Colonel Howie and that he was presently living comfortably in a flat in Budapest, presumably in possession of documents. Plans had already been made for Howie to be contacted and informed that A-Forces were waiting to guide him across the border. Gabor was of the opinion that at the present time, Howie would succeed in reaching Yugoslavia quickly. [27]

"I know Colonel Howie. He is living comfortably in a flat and is, I believe, now in possession of documents. It is

easy for Minnie to send on word that 'A' Forces are waiting to guide him across." [28]

Gabor Haraszty (ALBERT)

Following his conversation with Gabor, Reuven Dafni (GARY) was soon put in contact with Howie, who was informed of Reuven's work. Howie was expected to be helped across the border within the following ten days. [29]

Gabor informed Lawson of his discussions with Hannah Senesh and Reuven Dafni. He added that he had put Hannah Senesh - MINNIE - in touch with the Polish community in Hungary. [30]

"I have put MINNIE in touch with the Polish community who are very helpful." [31]

He reported that in Cazma, he had met EDEN and WILLIS (Sergeant Berdichev). EDEN had a lengthy discussion with him. [32]

He repeated what he had already told the parachutists in Yugoslavia – that pretending to be French was the most advisable approach for an agent or prisoner to take in Hungary. [33]

"The Hungarians do not permit the Germans to arrest the French, therefore agents and prisoners if they speak French should try and pose as Frenchmen who have escaped from France into Hungary." [34]

Gabor Haraszty (ALBERT)

When one had made it to Hungary, a good name to know was Charles Szladits, of the Commercial Bank in Budapest. Szladits was a very useful helper to the British, as he knew the position of all the prisoners. [35]

How to Escape

ALBERT reported that while the local currency in Hungary of pengoes were the best to have, they proved too bulky to carry. The most preferable gold coins were Napoleons. As far as paper money was concerned, dollar notes were the best option. He suggested high dollar notes, no less than 50 or 100 dollar bills. At the time of his report, the exchange rate was approximately 30 pengoes for one dollar. [36]

A good way to arrange the escape of an individual was by bribery. Hungarian officials at the time were easy to bribe, though one had to take care not to attempt to bribe very high officials and not to offer too large a bribe to the lower officials. For the escape of one individual from a prison camp, 500 pengoes was considered a sufficient bribe. [37]

The prison camps were not all that difficult to escape from (though military prisons were another matter altogether). Gabor pointed out that the real difficulty would occur after one managed to escape from a camp. He recommended that escapees get into civilian clothing as quickly as possible and then make their way to Budapest. He had found that 70% of the population in the capital were sympathetic toward the Allies. The Jewish population, due to the continual danger they were in, were generally not in a position to offer active assistance to escaped prisoners or evaders, but would never give away any prisoners who made contact with them. [38]

One could expect help from the working class, although the outsiders/escapers would not necessarily be able to find or recognize them. [39]

Gabor informed Lawson that taxi drivers offered a good possibility for escapers, as they were easily recognized and were familiar with the camps. And if one could reach any of the Polish camps around Budapest, one had a good chance.[40]

Of course, he added, to speak French was the most advisable thing to do. It would be the ideal cover.[41]

Downed airmen could expect to meet a number of helpers in Hungary and when they did, it was important to follow their instructions, as 30% of the population was still against the Allies, so there was still an element of danger.[42]

Gabor then warned that everyone should beware of any members of the fascist Arrow Cross party, who were easily distinguishable by the badges they wore. Upon completing his report, he drew two pictures of Arrow Cross insignias on the same page. One was a cross made with two arrows, the other a certain shaped letter V. As he was tired from his journey, his hand was not as steady as usual and one of the arrows drawn was slightly shorter than the other, though the dreaded symbols were still clear enough to recognize.[43]

He could not have known at the time that Hungary would fall under the control of the Arrow Cross in a matter of months.

MI9

R.S. Taylor and others on the MI9 staff at Bari were soon aware of ALBERT's work.[44]

The head of MI9 since 1941 had been Lieutenant-Colonel A.C. Simonds. "Tony" Simonds had a talent for intelligence. He had previously been in the Special Operations Executive (SOE) and so it was only natural that there was a certain amount of cooperation between MI6, MI9 and SOE on the field - though they were not without problems.[45] That same summer, for example, Simonds informed Taylor in a cipher message that he did not trust certain missions who wished to remove GARY (Reuven Dafni) from his current location. He was of the opinion that GARY should remain at the Yugoslav/Hungarian border, as he was their sole remaining representative who would be able to help those expected out of Hungary - instead of abandoning them, as other missions had suggested. [46]

Simonds was not the only high ranking British Officer aware of Gabor Haraszty's role in the London-Budapest game. When Captain Bowlby, head of ISLD (Cairo) was informed in June 1944 that a British agent had crossed from Hungary into Yugoslavia and was en route to Bari, he automatically assumed that the agent was ALBERT. [47]

MI9 was famous for its secret codes, invisible ink, hollow heels designed for carrying messages, flashlights containing secret messages, and agents of various identities. It was vital to make the false identification documents of agents as authentic as possible – before they were infiltrated into a country.

On June 23, 1944, the A-Force dispatched documents for delivery to GARY. They were copies of the reproduced identity document which had been supplied by ALBERT, the original having been returned the previous day. The method of creating the documents was explained in an enclosed letter in Hebrew. There were photographs, a rubber stamp, and details left for the agents to fill in. ALBERT's input was required as well. It was asked that ALBERT should have a look at the specimen copy they had made of his card, to complete any possible omissions that may have been made. The only thing the British were unable to obtain was the 2 pengoes stamp, which would need to be obtained at a post office in Hungary, as per ALBERT's suggestion. [47]

ALBERT and JONES (Perez Goldstein)

Earlier, a telegram had come through with a message that was to be passed to GARY. Though all of the other parachutists were to proceed as soon as possible, JONES was not to proceed to Hungary (OHIO) until ALBERT returned from Bari. JONES would be required to go into Hungary with ALBERT. He would be ALBERT's W/T operator. Further instructions would follow later. [48]

It was not surprising that Perez Goldstein (Jones) had been selected as Gabor Haraszty's radio operator, for both were agents of the Inter-Service Liaison Department (ISLD), while Joel Palgi and Hannah Senesh were listed as MI9 agents. [49]

Goldstein and Palgi were CHICKEN II operations. ALBERT operations, as would later be discovered by the enemy, were linked to CHICKEN II. [50]

Unfortunately, by the time the message was sent, JONES had already crossed into Hungary. [51]

Had the message arrived sooner, it would have reached him in time for him to wait for ALBERT. But as it had not, Perez Goldstein and Joel Palgi entered Hungary without Gabor Haraszty. Fate, it seemed, had other plans in store for everyone ...

Notes:

1. WO 208/3381 (see Albert's report)
2. Ibid
3. Y. Palgi, *Into the Inferno: the Memoir of a Jewish Paratrooper Behind Nazi Lines* (Rutgers University Press 2003)
4. i. F.S. Jones, *The Double Dutchman* (Corgi Books 1978)
   ii. HS 4/129
5. HS 9/753/2 *(SOE Personnel File of Howie)*
6. WO 208/3381 (see Albert's report)
7. Y. Palgi, *Into the Inferno: the Memoir of a Jewish Paratrooper Behind Nazi Lines* (Rutgers University Press 2003)
8. Ibid
9. WO 208/3381 (see Albert's report)
10. Y. Palgi, *Into the Inferno: the Memoir of a Jewish Paratrooper Behind Nazi Lines* (Rutgers University Press 2003)
11. *Torchlighters 2003*, (Yad Vashem Magazine 2004)
12. M.R.D. Foot & J.M. Langley, *MI9 Escape and Evasion 1939-1945* (Bodley Head 1979)
13. Y. Palgi, *Into the Inferno: the Memoir of a Jewish Paratrooper Behind Nazi Lines* (Rutgers University Press 2003)
14. WO 208/3381
15. i. M.R.D. Foot & J.M. Langley, *MI9 Escape and Evasion 1939-1945* (Bodley Head 1979)
    ii. WO 208/3401 *(MI9 personnel file of Anna Szenes)*
16. WO 208/3381 (see Albert's report)
17. WO 208/3405 *(MI9 personnel file of Nussbacher (Palgi), with reports)*
18. WO 208/3381 (see Albert's report)
19. Ibid
20. Ibid
21. Ibid
22. Y. Palgi, *Into the Inferno: the Memoir of a Jewish*

Paratrooper Behind Nazi Lines (Rutgers University Press 2003)
23. WO 208/3381
24. WO 208/3381
25. Y. Palgi, *Into the Inferno: the Memoir of a Jewish Paratrooper Behind Nazi Lines* (Rutgers University Press 2003)
26. WO 208/3381 (see Albert's report)
27. Ibid
28. Ibid
29. WO 208/3381
30. WO 208/3381 (see Albert's report)
31. Ibid
32. Ibid
33. Ibid
34. Ibid
35. Ibid
36. Ibid
37. Ibid
38. Ibid
39. Ibid
40. Ibid
41. Ibid
42. Ibid
43. Ibid
44. WO 208/3381
45. M.R.D. Foot & J.M. Langley, *MI9 Escape and Evasion 1939-1945* (Bodley Head 1979)
46. WO 208/3381
47. WO 208/3381
48. Ibid
49. Ibid
50. WO 208/3405 *(MI9 personnel file of Nussbacher (Palgi), with reports)*
51. Ibid

CHAPTER 8
ZIONISTS

From WO 208/3405

Excerpts from the signed Full Interrogation Report of Noah Nussbacher (Joel Palgi), a.k.a. MICKY, of "A" Forces Intelligence Section (M.I.9.)

"At the end of July they were brought back to HADIK prison, Budapest ...On the day after their arrival, the police arranged a meeting between JONES, NUSSBACHER, and STIPE. STIPE was asked by the police which of them was ALBERT, and he pointed to NUSSBACHER. (It appears that they were trying to find out which was the agent ALBERT, and STIPE knowing that NUSSBACHER's code name was HULBERT, evidently got the names mixed). The Hungarians decided that they had discovered the agent ALBERT, and so they started torturing NUSSBACHER again, and told him that they had evidence that NUSSBACHER had left Budapest a short time ago and had gone to the partisan area in Yugoslavia, and had returned again to Budapest.

After being tortured again, NUSSBACHER agreed to sign everything they wished him to about his being ALBERT, but decided that he would convince them at his trial that he was not ALBERT and that he had been forced to sign it ...

On 11th September, 1944, JONES and NUSSBACHER were again transferred to HADIK... In the corridor of the

*GESTAPO prison they met all those who had taken part in **CHICKEN I, CHICKEN II, and ALBERT operations**. This was the first time they had met HANNAH since their imprisonment, but they could not speak to her in the presence of the S.S."*

How it all Began …

While in Yugoslavia waiting to cross into Hungary, Joel Palgi (Nussbacher) received an urgent message from Headquarters that he was NOT to contact Joel Brand or Rudolf Kasztner. Unaware of the real reason for the order, he assumed that Brand had been arrested by the Gestapo. [1]

By then, however, the Hungarian partisan Major (STIPE) had already learned that Kasztner and Brand were two of Joel Palgi's contacts in Budapest. Palgi had passed a letter for him to have delivered to Brand in Budapest and had given him the Budapest address of both Joel Brand and Rudolf Kasztner. Unbeknownst to Palgi at the time, the Hungarian partisan Major had then asked the other Tito partisans who Brand and Kasztner were, thus informing a number of people that they were Palgi's contacts. [2]

STIPE had also promised to take Palgi's party across the border.[3]

Agents Palgi, Goldstein and Rosenfeld (a.k.a. Dickens) slowly made their way toward the Hungarian border. The journey had already been delayed – too many times. The partisan Major, who had previously agreed to get them into Hungary, had temporarily disappeared. [4]

Palgi soon located him, but he did not have any promising news. The partisan warned them that a Croatian fascist unit was already aware of British Officers penetrating Hungary from Croatia and they had sent agents to the border to watch for them. It was therefore too dangerous to cross. [5]

Palgi and his party communicated this information to Cairo, but received no reply. In addition, they asked the partisans to supply them with a courier to send a message to CHICKEN I, including Hannah Senesh, warning them of the situation. The partisans refused. [6]

After a while, Palgi and Goldstein were able to proceed with the partisan Major, who was still their only option. Rosenfeld was no longer with them, as Eden had ordered him back to Kalnik, to await documents that they were then expecting Hannah to send. [7]

On June 17, Palgi and Goldstein were informed by Eden that the British Officers of another mission in the area had cabled Cairo that they suspected Palgi and his party were traitors. This, Eden explained, had led the fascist intelligence to discover their plan to enter Hungary. In addition, the Political Commissar of the partisans had complained to Eden that sending Jewish refugees from Hungary to the partisan territory would hinder the war effort of the partisans. [8]

Palgi did not find Eden entirely supportive of their mission. [9]

The situation of the Jewish parachutists was increasingly difficult. They became more determined than ever to do whatever they had to in order to reach Hungary and carry out their work.

On June 19, Palgi and Goldstein finally managed to cross the Drava River. As it would not have been possible to take the W/T set with them, they left it in the care of a friend of the partisan Major. The partisan Major was certain his friend was reliable. He agreed to have the suitcase containing the W/T set and batteries delivered at the railway station in Kaposvar - 3 hours from Budapest - on June 26. Someone would be able to pick it up from there and deliver it to Palgi. [10]

The partisan Major's contacts, whom they soon met in Hungary, did not seem trustworthy. As there was no other prospect in sight, Palgi and Goldstein proceeded with them. Their suspicions later proved justified, for three of the

Hungarian partisans they had met at the border were in fact Hungarian agents. [11]

BUDAPEST
Danger

Palgi and Goldstein eventually parted company with the "partisans." They got to Budapest in the early morning of June 23. Once there, they called one of their contacts and were informed he had been arrested by the Gestapo shortly after the German occupation. Palgi then telephoned Rudolf Kasztner for help and was told by his wife that he would not be home until the afternoon. [12]

Kasztner, a Jewish Hungarian lawyer and an old friend, was one of the leaders of the Jewish Aid and Rescue Committee. He had met with Oscar Schindler in late 1942. [13]
He himself was in the midst of finalizing a deal with the Nazis – a deal which Eichmann had proposed concerning a rescue train. It was a prelude of sorts to the bigger proposal which everyone assumed Joel Brand was already negotiating with the Allies.

It was not safe to wander the streets of German-occupied Budapest. Palgi went to buy cinema tickets for himself and Goldstein. At least in the cinema, they would remain out of sight. They arranged to rendezvous in an hour at the Nemzeti Cinema. As it turned out, there was also a restaurant by the same name. This caused a little confusion and Goldstein first went to the restaurant. Later, when Goldstein and Palgi finally did meet, it was too late as the cinema tickets had expired. [14]
Meanwhile, unbeknownst to them, they were already being shadowed by the Hungarian police. The agent following them had bought a cinema ticket corresponding to the time of Palgi's tickets and, assuming both men would show up at the

cinema at the allotted time, went off to have lunch. When he returned, he found that neither Palgi nor Goldstein had entered the cinema and assumed that he had been tricked with a tactic of British intelligence. [15]

That afternoon, Palgi and Goldstein met with Dr. Kasztner in his flat at the Corso Pension. Kasztner was startled to see them. He spoke of the difficulty of the current situation for the Jewish population and how he was anxiously awaiting the return of Joel Brand. He informed them of Eichmann's proposal. [16]

Joel Palgi was skeptical about the Brand deal – and rightfully so. As they would later learn, Joel Brand had already been arrested by British Intelligence and taken to Cairo, where he was interrogated for hours every day. Furthermore, the British had no intention of letting him return to Budapest. [17]

Kasztner also informed Palgi and Goldstein of the rescue train and explained that things were almost in place. He was actively preparing for the departure of what would come to be known as the Kasztner train - a transport of over 1600 Jews who were to be taken by train out of Nazi-occupied Hungary. It too was a costly, albeit controversial deal. Kurt Becher had to be paid approximately one thousand dollars in assets including cash, jewelry, and gold - per passenger.

The fact that two British Officers who were Jewish Palestinians had just arrived in Budapest seemed to make Kasztner nervous. What if the Nazis found out? It would put the entire arrangement in jeopardy. [18]

But the reality was that they were there – and they were not about to turn back.

In Nazi occupied Budapest, Palgi and Goldstein found themselves in a hostile terrain where deportations were underway and it was next to impossible to make a move. They had ventured to Hungary to set up escape routes and organize underground activities. They were not about to give up on their mission.

Kasztner agreed to help them find a place to stay. They ended up at the Hotel Adria and got to work, meeting with the Jewish Underground, but soon realized they were being followed by Hungarian agents. [19]

Kasztner was tipped off that they were going to be arrested as British spies, so he took matters into his own hands and went directly to the Gestapo with a story to cover for the pair. He told the Germans that two Jewish envoys had arrived in Budapest in connection with the negotiations for the Brand case. [20]

The Germans requested that Kasztner send the two envoys to see them and said they would not allow the Hungarian police to arrest them. [21]

Palgi and Goldstein decided to wait for 24 hours. In the meantime, the Corso, where Kasztner lived, was raided by the Hungarian police. The police were looking for two men. Time was running out … [22]

GESTAPO

Palgi and Goldstein decided that Palgi should be the one to present himself to the Gestapo and attempt to bluff his way through their questions, as he was the more experienced and older of the two. Goldstein was to remain on the outside, just in case… [23]

Palgi headed for the Gestapo and introduced himself as a Jewish envoy. The clerk advised him to return the next day and report to Colonel Klages. The next day he did just that. However, Colonel Klages was still not in, so a Gestapo Officer took Palgi's statement, as per Klages' instructions. [24]

His story was that he had been sent by Jewish authorities to negotiate with the Nazis and had paid a British Officer 2000 pound sterling to take him to Yugoslavia by plane, after which he had crossed into Hungary. He pretended he had lost contact with the other envoy, with whom he had arrived. He added that he was there to negotiate on behalf of the Jewish side in the Joel Brand-Eichmann case. [25]

The Gestapo Officer informed him he was free to leave the building and gave him a Gestapo telephone number to call, in the event that the Hungarians should try to arrest him. [26]

Palgi then returned to the empty flat of Joel Brand, where he was now staying. [27]

YUGOSLAVIA

On June 24, 1944, Reuven Dafni (GARY) reported that unfortunately, no news had been heard from Hannah Senesh (MINNIE) since her departure to Hungary. Contact with Hungary was proving extremely difficult, owing to an unexpected large scale offensive in the Kalnik area of Yugoslavia. Shortly afterwards, the partisans experienced a setback. Thus, for the time being there was no chance at all of crossing into Hungary, much less re-establishing radio contact ... [28]

ARRESTS

On June 27, a Hungarian Officer marched into Joel Brand's Budapest flat, accompanied by a Gestapo Officer. The Hungarian Officer announced he was there to arrest Joel Palgi. Palgi pretended to become indignant and stated he was making a mistake. The Gestapo Officer refused to help despite the fact that the Gestapo had previously said they would not allow any such arrest to take place. [29]

What had changed?

As luck would have it, by that time, Palgi's radio set had arrived and fallen into the hands of the Hungarian police, so they were aware that in reality, he had penetrated Hungary for an Allied military organization. And they now had proof.[30]

He was arrested and taken to the Hungarian Military Prison in Budapest (Hadik), where Military counter-espionage proceeded to interrogate him. They demanded to know where JONES (Goldstein) was. Palgi refused to answer and was tortured. A prison guard told him Hannah Senesh had also been captured and brought to the same prison. It was devastating news. [31]

Palgi was later moved to the notorious Gestapo prison on Fo Street (Utca). The Gestapo had managed to intercept a copy of the MI9 Chicken I signal plan. They were all in grave danger. However, the enemy seemed unaware of any agents' real identities. They were also not aware of the fact that Palgi's code name was HULBERT. [32]

The police had additional plans in store and transported Palgi back to Hadik Military Prison in July. There, they placed him in a cell with the now captured Goldstein, and the arrested partisan Major who had helped them cross the border. [33]

The three men waited for their next move.

The interrogator addressed the partisan Major. "Which one of them is ALBERT?" [34]

Without hesitation, the partisan Major pointed to Joel Palgi, whose code name was in fact HULBERT, not ALBERT. [35]

The Gestapo and Hungarian counter-espionage were now convinced that Palgi was British agent ALBERT.
They tortured him and demanded a confession. [36]

They claimed to have evidence that the British agent known as ALBERT had recently crossed from Hungary into Yugoslavia through the Tito partisans and then returned to Budapest. They had also linked Chicken Operations to Albert Operations. [37]

In fact, Chicken operations and Albert operations were connected, for the plan had been that the Jewish Palestinian Officers would assist Allied airmen who had become POWs and they would also rescue Jews.
Hence ALBERT's planned involvement.

The torture was unbearable. Palgi "confessed" that yes, he was indeed ALBERT, to make them stop, and agreed to sign whatever they put in front of him. [38]

The best course of action, it appeared, would be to wait until his trial, at which time he would prove to them that they were dead wrong about his identity ... [39]

Meanwhile, the communist informers among the prison guards continued to observe and pass on information about what was going on around them. [40]

Notes:

1. WO 208/3405 *(MI9 personnel file of Nussbacher (Palgi), with reports)*
2. Ibid
3. Ibid
4. Ibid
5. Ibid
6. Ibid
7. Ibid
8. Ibid
9. Ibid
10. Ibid
11. Ibid
12. Ibid
13. Kasztner Memorial Site
14. WO 208/3405 *(MI9 personnel file of Nussbacher (Palgi), with reports)*
15. Ibid
16. Ibid
17. Alex Weissberg, *Desperate Mission: Joel Brand's Story* (Criterion Books 1958)

18. WO 208/3405 *(MI9 personnel file of Nussbacher (Palgi), with reports)*
19. Ibid
20. Ibid
21. Ibid
22. Ibid
23. Ibid
24. Ibid
25. Ibid
26. Ibid
27. Ibid
28. WO 208/3381
29. WO 208/3405 *(MI9 personnel file of Nussbacher (Palgi), with reports)*
30. Ibid
31. Ibid
32. Ibid
33. Ibid
34. Ibid
35. Ibid
36. Ibid
37. Ibid
38. Ibid
39. Ibid
40. Y. Palgi, *Into the Inferno: the Memoir of a Jewish Paratrooper Behind Nazi Lines* (Rutgers University Press 2003)

CHAPTER 9
THE NEIGHBORHOOD OF RAOUL WALLENBERG

Budapest - Autumn 1944

The Danube River flows through Budapest at a very fast pace. Anyone who looks into it for a long period of time will notice how alive and vibrant it is, though the murky waters appear to be pulled in different turbulent directions. The river separates the Buda side of Budapest from the Pest side and is traversed by a number of bridges. The Chain Bridge, whose stone lion statues provide a regal, somewhat territorial greeting to outsiders, is the most famous one.

Gellert Hill in Buda is connected to downtown Budapest by the fin-de-siecle Independence Bridge, with mythical turul birds on the top. Not far from the Pest side of the bridge, in 1944, stood the Gestapo Headquarters, a stark reminder that Hungary was currently under German occupation. No one was reminded more of this fact than the Jewish citizens of Hungary, whose lives hung in the balance.

On the Buda side of the Independence bridge, however, there was hope - in a place called Gellert Hill.

At the bottom of the hill were two majestic sites. The Gellert Hotel was a spa hotel which had been built on the banks of the Danube in 1918, with ornate rooms, grand architecture, and well known thermal springs. Nearby was the Cave Church (Sziklatemplom), a chapel which the Paulist order had built in a natural cave on the side of the hill - modeled after Lourdes.

Further up the hill were paths, secluded, densely treed lots, winding roads, and elegant villas. After climbing the hill for approximately ten minutes, one arrived at an imposing, spacious villa with a long line of people standing in front. The line was so long that it extended far down the street from the villa. This was the Swedish Embassy, where diplomat Raoul Wallenberg worked long hours with his small staff. The men and women in line, clutching whatever documents they had, were waiting for their chance to obtain Schutzpasses. [1]

It was a place of hope.

Just across the Swedish Embassy was the Finnish Legation, which was also used by the Swedes, and next door to the Finnish Legation stood yet another villa – the family home of Karoly Schandl.

In Nazi occupied Budapest in 1944, Swedish diplomat Raoul Wallenberg was Karoly Schandl's neighbor.

Raoul Wallenberg had arrived in Budapest in July of that year, just after Karoly had been reactivated as a reservist in the Hungarian army, and just after he'd taken a Jewish friend home to hide. [2]

Karoly Schandl lived at 16-18 Kelenhegyi Street. The Finnish Legation was at 20 Kelenhegyi. Karoly had his own apartment on the second floor of the family villa, with a private entrance. It was here that he secretly brought his Jewish friend Kari, the day before he was supposed to be deported. Karoly had met him at the Basilica, removed the yellow star from his jacket, and insisted he return home with him. Kari was like a younger brother to him and so he hid him in the secret closet in his upstairs apartment and took him food every day. [3]

Terezia Schandl, Karoly's mother, soon discovered he had a mysterious guest. She insisted he join them for family dinners and, for his protection, procured a robe of the Paulist monks for him to wear as a disguise. The robe was given to the Schandls by the priests of the Cave Church, for they too were against the Nazis, and were close to the Schandl family.

Karoly Schandl Sr. and his wife Terezia were religious

Roman Catholics. Terezia was active in five charities and soon became involved in helping the Jewish population. [4]

As she would later state in her memoirs :

*During those difficult times I had been active in volunteer work, and was on the board of **5 charitable organizations:***

Association of Villages (Faluszövetség)

Charitable Association of Women in Buda (Budai Jótékony Nőegylet)

Lisieux Saint Teréz Residence and Food bank (Lisieuxi Szent Teréz Menza és Kollégium)

Bokreta Street Home for Working Women (Bokréta Utcai Munkásnők Otthona)

Retirement Home for Women Civil Servants (Tisztviselő telepi Urinők Otthona).

I did my best to help the less fortunate during those difficult and trying times.

One morning, someone wearing a yellow star was looking for me. I recognized the young woman – she was one of the hairdressers from my hair salon. Her name was Ilus. She fell to her knees and begged me, sobbing, to help her. Her husband was taken to the front lines by the Nazis for forced labor. I lifted her up, tore off the hated yellow star from her coat, put it in my pocket, and eventually burned it. I promised to help her if she swore to keep her identity a secret. When she did, I chose her a new name and told her that she could stay in our house until I got her papers with her new identity.

I found a suitable escape story in my notebook for Ilus, and for the time being, I had her hide in our home. Budapest in those days was a haven for Erdelyi (Transylvanian) refugees. Thousands fled Erdely and came to Budapest. They traveled by train, by wagon, some even walked. I had a girlfriend in Budapest whose entire family lived in various regions in Erdely. She and her relatives who arrived in Budapest told me numerous stories of their escape, describing in detail the routes they took, etc. I wrote down these stories in a notebook, including the escape routes, and used the stories later for the persons I obtained false papers for. They were each given a true escape story (as if it was their own) with the false papers, so as to lend authenticity to their new identity.

The Finnish Embassy was our next door neighbor. One of the entrances to their garden was next to our villa's entrance. At the same entrance, around the clock, stood Hungarian police guards who were assigned to the Embassy. During cold days in the winter, I sent them hot drinks to warm up and during the hot summer days, I used to send them cool drinks. As the men were not protected from the elements, I also gave them permission to stand in our garage during rainy days, from where they could still see the entrance to the Embassy. As we had a good relationship with the guards, they brought me the files (lists) of the new Transylvanian refugees from the police station. [5]

The Finnish Legation next door was actually being used by the Swedes – and it was also where Raoul Wallenberg was hiding 30 Jewish Hungarians. [6]

The Underground

Karoly had been active in the British-Hungarian underground for quite some time. He helped gather intelligence and also escorted escaped Allied prisoners of war to the Yugoslav border. There were monthly deliveries to be made and monthly reports to deliver to the Center. The POWs and reports were delivered via the Tito partisans, who saw to it that all were forwarded to Bari by the monthly supply plane. On the way back to Bari, the transport planes carried special cargo – detailed reports and escaped prisoners of war. Karoly was one of the messengers who delivered the Allied "spies" and reports to the Croatian border, as directed by Churchill's Special Operations Executive. The British Secret Intelligence Service and the Special Operations Executive were working together. [7]

At the same time, Karoly was a Lieutenant in the Hungarian army, having been activated in the Reserves. He was a lecturer and tactical adjutant with the H.Q. of Hungarian Defensive Air Forces. It was the ideal cover for his other activities. And no one would have guessed that a Hungarian officer close to becoming a captain was hiding a Jewish friend in his apartment. [8]

Gabor Haraszty (ALBERT) was a frequent visitor to Karoly's home. It had taken him longer than anticipated to return from the Allies yet when he had, it was with even more enthusiasm for the British.

His activities continued, despite the fact that Budapest was swarming with spies, informers and rumors that hindered ease of movement. He remained completely underground in the capital, though his close friends were in constant contact with him. He continued to use the British intelligence radio in his family villa to receive and transmit messages.[9] His friend Peter Zerkowitz also used the radio to communicate with the Allies.

Karoly trusted his friend implicitly and did everything possible to help him. The servants had instructions to allow Gabor Haraszty to enter his apartment at any time of the day or night, whether or not Karoly was present. There were meetings of the underground held in Karoly Schandl's apartment - and sometimes those meetings with Gabor were attended by Swedish diplomat Raoul Wallenberg.

Notes:

1. Gabor Forgacs, *the History of the Wallenberg Office hired by the Swedish Embassy* (see Raoul Wallenberg Association, France 2004)
2. C. Schandl, *Sword of the Turul* (Lulu Press 2005)
3. Ibid
4. Ibid
5. Ibid
6. Ibid
7. Ibid
8. Ibid
9. Ibid

CHAPTER 10
SECRET NEGOTIATIONS

Budapest – September 1944

Colonel Howie was still in Hungary. His plans had changed a number of times. Arrangements had been made in the previous months to have him transported across the Hungarian/Yugoslav border by a British agent in contact with Reuven Dafni, but the journey had been called off.

Earlier that year, the outspoken South African colonel had informed Captain Roy Natusch he'd decided not to go to Yugoslavia – after Natusch expressed his belief he would be able to secure safe passage to the Tito partisans. Howie had felt he still had work to do in Budapest. [1]

A great deal had happened since then. At the end of July, Horthy's son – whom Howie had first met through Prince Sapieha – took Howie to see Regent Horthy at the Royal Palace. It was the first of numerous meetings. [2]

During the meetings, Howie attempted to convince Regent Horthy to surrender to the Russians. Horthy refused, stating that to surrender to the Russians would be tantamount to stabbing his countrymen in the back. Also present were General Naday, Horthy's Attaché Tost, as well as Count Bethlen. Since the German occupation of Hungary, Count Bethlen had once more become a man of influence in Hungarian politics. He remained in hiding and his visits to the Palace were clandestine, like those of the South African Colonel. [3]

In early September, Horthy agreed to make contact with the Anglo-Americans. Thus, Count Bethlen and the Chief of Staff set about drafting a letter to the Anglo-Americans, to help Hungary break away from the Germans. Howie, who by then had been provided with an apartment in the Palace, was given a W/T set, which was placed in the room above his. Communication was made with the Polish HQ in London every Monday and Thursday. [4]

When Count Bethlen and the Chief of Staff had finished the letter, Howie's radio operator was unable to transmit any message. It was impossible to make contact, even through the WARSAW line. [5]

Meanwhile, the Gestapo complained that they were picking up strange signals from the Royal Palace. The Hungarians insisted the radio communications be stopped. It was simply too risky. [6]

Alternative arrangements were made for the letter to be transported to the Allies. It would be sent to Switzerland by courier, where it was to be handed over to Bakos Hessenye - and "onward transmission." The courier was dispatched. In addition, a copy of the same message was given to the Hungarian Military Attaché who was about to proceed to Stockholm. The message would then be transmitted from Stockholm to London. [7]

As it was now too dangerous for Howie and his Polish entourage to remain in the Palace, they were smuggled out to a waiting car, which took them to a house near Lake Balaton. They attempted to contact London by radio again, but had no success. A thunderstorm was making communications difficult. [8]

They did, however, receive a message from Budapest – that the Gestapo was on their track. As a result, Howie and his entourage were quickly moved to Esztergom. The Polish party soon decided to venture to Slovakia, to join the Polish Forces there. Before they left, Colonel Tost arrived. He convinced Howie to return to the capital with him. [9]

Back in Budapest, Howie conferred with Horthy's son and Tost, who agreed to evacuate the colonel by plane. It took three days to arrange the transport, during which time Howie was hidden on the island of Csepel. A police contact soon arrived to inform him that all was ready. [10]

Reginald Barratt was among the men who escorted Colonel Howie on his journey from Csepel Island. Barratt's close contact with the Colonel is not surprising. He had been one of three men who had been chosen among the POWs at Szigetvar to help prepare for the Allied landing Howie had told Roy Natusch to expect. [11]

That had been several months earlier – and that mission had been aborted. Some said it had been a matter of bad timing, as the German invasion had prevented it. But it was later said that the British had abandoned the idea as Stalin had disagreed with it.

Howie was taken to the awaiting Heinkel 111 aircraft. The passengers included Naday, Howie, a Hungarian pilot and his wife, in addition to a Hungarian mechanic. [12]

Howie insisted they fly directly to Italy, though the Hungarians would have preferred neutral territory. After a fearful crash landing near Termoli, the group was shaken up, but miraculously, all survived. [13]

From there, the Americans drove the group to Bari. They spent the night at 15th Air Force H.Q., and the next day were promptly flown to Air Force Headquarters. Colonel Howie's Hungarian involvement had come to an end, though he would later receive the Order of the British Empire for his efforts. [14]

HORTHY'S ACCOUNT

After The March invasion of Hungary by the Nazis, Hungary's situation had become a nightmare.

Tragically, Eichmann and his murderous campaign got underway, as hundreds of thousands of Jewish citizens were deported.

The Germans had installed spies everywhere, to help pave the way. One was Peter Hain, the personal inspector of

Horthy, who soon moved his office into the Majestic Hotel, organized the arrests of high-ranking individuals, interfered in politics – and had close contact with Eichmann. [15]

Hain helped implement the deportations. [16]

By August, there were 170,000 Jews registered in Budapest, while 110,000 Jewish Hungarians remained hidden by friends. Regent Horthy stated in his memoirs that in August 1944, he informed the government of the Reich that he himself intended to prevent the removal of the remaining Jewish Hungarians in Budapest and for this reason the Germans did not take "further measures." [17]

WALLENBERG

The attempts of the Raoul Wallenberg Mission to allow the Jews unhindered passage to Palestine was also known by Regent Horthy. [18]

In the first week of August 1944, Horthy spoke with Raoul Wallenberg and requested that the Swedish diplomat write up some anonymous suggestions for him concerning actions which might be taken. Wallenberg did write up the suggestions and presented them to the Regent. They included a request that individuals with collective passports should not be required to wear the Star of David and that the clergy should be permitted to "speak their mind." [19]

It is not known to what extent Horthy listened to Wallenberg's suggestions. Colonel Howie had described the Regent as a man who was always influenced the most by the last person he had seen; hence his apparent indecision.

THE PRO-ANGLO-AMERICAN HUNGARIANS

By early September, it became evident that Soviet armored divisions would soon reach Hungary.

Horthy summoned Count Stephen (Istvan) Bethlen to the Palace in order to seek his advice. Bethlen, who had eluded his ordered arrest by the German secret police, was in hiding outside the capital. On September 10, Bethlen secretly attended a meeting at the Palace, which included Horthy, as well as a number of trusted Hungarians and aristocrats. In all, there were 12 secret counselors. Count Bethlen proposed an attempt at ending the war, to stop the bloodshed. There was unanimous agreement in the room. [21]

When Bethlen later took his leave of the Palace, it was without his moustache, which had been shaved off to prevent anyone from recognizing him. [22]

As Horthy would later write in his memoirs, on September 22, he sent General Naday and Colonel Howie to Allied Headquarters in Italy. General Naday, who was pro-British, had long believed in an Allied victory. [23]

Upon arriving in Caserta, Naday conferred with British General Sir Henry Maitland Wilson and Air Marshal Sir John Cotesworth Slessor. He was informed by both men that they were powerless to act - that it was necessary that Hungary communicate with the Russians. [24]

This statement foreshadowed, on a different scale, what was to become of the idealistic Gabor Haraszty and his friends, for they too would be ordered to report to the Russians.

In the end of September, the next steps were carried out by a reluctant Horthy, who still viewed Russia as the enemy and feared that the communist regime would pillage and conquer Hungary. He sent Hungary's former military attaché in Moscow back to the city, along with four trusted representatives, to negotiate an armistice. [25]

They had hoped to achieve an immediate end to the

hostilities, British and American involvement in the inevitable occupation of Hungary, and a withdrawal of German troops. Negotiations began with the Russians, who demanded that any armistice should be effective as of October 16. It seemed they wished to speed things up before the Americans had a chance to take part. The Americans had already complained of being left out of certain negotiations between Churchill and Joseph Stalin. [26]

Unbeknownst to Regent Horthy, Count Bethlen, various groups in the Hungarian resistance, and the Hungarians the British continued to use for intelligence purposes, there was never going to be a free Hungary. On October 11, 1944, Foreign Secretary Anthony Eden and Molotov had decided on the percentage figures of Allied involvement in Balkan countries after the war. Hungary was to find itself 80% Russian-controlled, while 20% would be the influence of "others." This was the final balance. Thus, by early October, it was known that Hungary was to be under the Russian sphere of influence. [27]

It soon became quite clear that the Germans had learned of the Hungarians' clandestine contact with the Allies. So swift and well coordinated was the Nazis' counter-attack that even Major-General Bakay, the commander of the troops in Budapest, was caught off guard. Horthy had entrusted Bakay to come up with a plan, in the event that the Palace would come under attack by the Germans. On October 8, however, Bakay was abducted by the Gestapo while stepping out of his car. [28]

Nicholas Horthy Jr., the Regent's son, was set up by the Gestapo, beaten senseless by 15 of their men, and abducted. He was to later become a pawn against Horthy during the darkest of times. [29]

ARMISTICE

On Monday October 15, 1944, Regent Horthy proceeded according to plan and made a live announcement on Radio Budapest. [30]

In his proclamation, he stated that

- Hungary had been forced into the war against the Allies by German pressure.

- In March, the Germans had invaded Hungary.

- It was evident the German Reich had lost the war.

-The Gestapo had acted in a manner that was incompatible with the demands of humanity.

- Hungary was about to conclude an armistice with her *previous enemies* and would cease all hostilities against them.

Horthy's attempts at an armistice, however, were already being sabotaged. The Arrow Cross fascist party had preparations in plan – to seize power. Meanwhile, German Tiger tanks patrolled the streets of Budapest. [31]

By the same afternoon, Arrow Cross leader Ferenc Szalasi managed to take over the airwaves as well, and his own speech was broadcast. Regent Horthy soon found himself under German "protective custody." His Palace apartment was ransacked and looted. [32]

Colonel Tost committed suicide in lieu of facing a lengthy Gestapo interrogation. [33]

Horthy was informed that the fascist Szalasi was to be the new Premier of Hungary. He was handed a sheet of paper announcing his abdication and declaring that Szalasi was the newly appointed Premier. His son was threatened with death.

The Regent signed at the bottom of the page. [34]

Horthy and his family were quickly transported to Schloss Hirschberg in Germany. One hundred Waffen-SS men patrolled the outside garden, while inside there were Gestapo men with guard dogs. His son was in the Mauthausen concentration camp, where he would remain until the war's end. [35]

Horthy would never see Hungarian soil again.

Notes:

1. F.S. Jones, *The Double Dutchman* (Corgi Books 1978)
2. HS 9/753/2 *(SOE Personnel File of Howie)*
3. Ibid
4. Ibid
5. Ibid
6. Ibid
7. Ibid
8. Ibid
9. Ibid
10. Ibid
11. F.S. Jones, *The Double Dutchman* (Corgi Books 1978)
12. HS 9/753/2 *(SOE Personnel File of Howie)*
13. Ibid
14. Ibid
15. *Eichmann Trial Transcripts* (Nizkor Project)

16. Hermann Krumey's Testimony, *Eichmann Trial Transcripts* (Nizkor Project)
17. A. Simon, Miklos Horthy, *Annotated Memoirs of Admiral Miklos Horthy, The Regent of Hungary* (1996)
18. Ibid
19. Raoul Wallenberg, *Letters and Dispatches 1924-1944* (Arcade Publishing 1996)
20. HS 9/753/2 *(SOE Personnel File of Howie)*
21. A. Simon, Miklos Horthy, *Annotated Memoirs of Admiral Miklos Horthy, The Regent of Hungary* (1996)
22. Ibid
23. Ibid
24. Ibid
25. Ibid
26. Ibid
27. Stephen Kertesz, *From the Second Vienna Award to Paris: Transylvania and Hungarian-Rumanian Relations During World War II* (in *The Roots of Ethnic Conflict*, Kent State University Press, 1983)
28. A. Simon, Miklos Horthy, *Annotated Memoirs of Admiral Miklos Horthy, The Regent of Hungary* (1996)
29. Ibid
30. Ibid
31. Ibid
32. Ibid
33. Ibid
34. Ibid
35. Ibid

CHAPTER 11
CHAOS IN BUDAPEST

Peter Zerkowitz, a good friend of both Karoly Schandl and Gabor Haraszty, had been arrested and taken to the military prison. Like most who passed through its doors, he was beaten. Peter had been arrested at the Officer's Club in Budapest, with fake IDs in his pocket, which he had been preparing to hand over to Szent-Miklosy of the Hungarian resistance (the Hungarian Independence Movement/MFM).[1] Nothing could be done to obtain his release. The military prison, unlike the Polish internment camp, could have only been influenced by the Head of State.

It was to be a dark time in Hungarian history. The pro-German Arrow Cross fascist party had seized control of the country. In the elections of 1939, they had won 30 seats in Parliament but the party was banned when the war broke out. They managed to remain underground, festering and waiting for the opportunity to re-emerge. That moment had come and the Germans had made their leader Ferenc Szalasi the new Prime Minister and Head of State.

Hungary's Jewish population was in continuous danger. Deportations began and there were arrests and atrocities committed at their Headquarters at 60 Andrassy Street, *which, ironically, would later house the Communist Secret police (AVO/AVH).*

The Arrow Cross must have suspected that there was some clandestine activity at the Schandl villa, for they frequently walked up to the house on Kelenhegyi Street and attempted to search the premises. Fortunately, as Karoly was a Lieutenant in the Hungarian Reserves, it was possible to keep them at bay. [2]

His Jewish friend Kari's situation was extremely precarious and he remained at Karoly's apartment, disguised as a Paulist monk/priest. Only the fathers and brothers of the Cave Church (Sziklatemplom) down the street knew that he really was not. They played an active role in helping Hungary's Jewish citizens, as well as members of the underground, some of whom were considered "helpers" of the British. [3]

It was a dangerous time to be in the anti-Nazi resistance. Karoly, Gabor and the others who were in the group were unaware that the Hungarian counter-intelligence had known of the existence of the British agent ALBERT since the summer.

It wasn't just ALBERT.

The Hungarian interrogators of suspected British agents were also trying to learn the exact location of the Buda villa of the mysterious "Uncle Karoly," who was known to be helping the Allies. [4] "Uncle Karoly" was either a reference to Charles - Karoly - Szladits, who managed a villa with Raphael Rupert where Allied POWs were hiding - or it was a reference to Karoly Schandl Senior. Fortunately, the real identity of "Uncle Karoly" in Buda was never discovered.

Meanwhile, Joel Palgi, Hannah Senesh, and Perez Goldstein were still imprisoned. Joel Palgi and Perez Goldstein's trials were postponed - but Hannah Senesh, who had been brutally tortured for radio codes, was suddenly executed. It was devastating news. There had been no sentence pronounced - just a sudden and senseless execution.

Even in death, her spirit continued to inspire.

Hannah would later become a folk hero, famous for both her courage and her writings.

While in Hadik prison, aware that the end was near, in her death cell she would write

> *"I could have been*
> *twenty-three next July;*
> *I gambled on what mattered most,*
> *The dice were cast. I lost."* [5]

THE WRONG MAN

Though the details are not clear, shortly after Hannah Senesh's unexpected murder, "the group" (which had been organized by Jacques/Jack Dubreuil and was now frequently led by Gabor) was planning to free two British agents – and were confident they would be able to procure their release.

It was apparently arranged via Jack's contacts in the Polish Underground.

Two men were expected, though on November 13, only one arrived - "Daniels." And Clement seemed to think he was the wrong one. [6]

Who were the 2 agents they had really been expecting?
On November 14, 1944, Perez Goldstein was sent to Komarom and from there to Germany. He was never seen again. [7]

Meanwhile Joel Palgi remained in prison.

On November 13, the sprung British agent, Daniels, had been sent to the Schandl villa, to hide in Karoly's apartment. How had Daniels arrived in Budapest? He had taken leave of his assigned mission at the Hungarian/Slovak border and ventured to the Hungarian capital. *Interestingly, the National Archives have categorized that mission under the Special Operations Executive (SOE) collection which includes*

Poland.

Once in Budapest, he was soon arrested and transported to Hadik prison, then to Zugliget.

After his release from Zugliget, the Polish internment camp near the homes of both Schandl and Haraszty, Daniels was taken to the Cave Church. He was then disguised as a Paulist monk, and taken to the Schandl villa.

According to Karoly, it was "the group" that had sent Daniels to his home.

Interestingly, one of Daniels' reports states that after his arrival in Zugliget prison, a British Officer in his small party made contact with the Polish underground to have him sprung from the camp, after which he was taken to the Schandls. [8]

It was Jack who was part of the Polish underground.

Thus, Jack had likely been involved in sending Daniels to Karoly's home.

But Daniels' escape might have been planned even before his arrival in Zugliget, if one considers the role of a certain Hungarian colonel.

GARZULY

As later stated by Joel Brand, Rudolf Kasztner had been in contact with Lieutenant Colonel Garcoly (Garzuly) of the Hungarian Secret Service. [9]

Kasztner had assumed that all it would take for Hannah Senesh, Perez Goldstein, and Joel Palgi to be released would be a phone call to his contact Garcoly. [10]

On October 14, Otto Komoly and Kasztner were finally promised the release of the three parachutists - but the Arrow Cross/SS putsch the following day changed everything. [11]

There were no releases. [12]

In fact, as Joel Palgi later reported to his British superiors, Colonel Garcoly had ignored him when he had complained to him in Hadik prison that he was being tortured. Garcoly reportedly ignored the marks on Palgi's body and did not listen to him. [13]

Garcoly did, however, come to the assistance of another party of British officers in Hadik prison, which included Lieutenant Daniels. A document in the U.K. National Archives praised the Hungarian colonel for having aided Daniels' party - and recommended him for a reward. *Garzuly was later reported to have been taken away by the Germans.* [14]

According to the British, Garzuly had been "partly responsible" for helping members of Daniels' party out of Hadik prison, after which time they were sent to Zugliget camp. Garzuly had been involved in arranging for their transfer to Zugliget. [15]

Once Daniels' party was at Zugliget, the British officer to whom he reported made contact with the Polish underground to arrange their release. It was then that Daniels was sent to the Schandl villa, released ahead of his comrades. And as later reported by the British, a Polish officer had been responsible for arranging Daniels' "escape." [16]

AT THE SCHANDL VILLA

Daniels is reported to have shown up at the Schandl villa on November 13, 1944. [17]

Documents in the U.K. National Archives indicate that during his stay in Budapest, the Allies had no communication with him. This is curious, considering that Karoly Schandl was known to have been involved in the British-led resistance, who had radio contact with Bari. All Daniels would have had to do is ask to transmit or have a message transmitted, yet for reasons unknown, he apparently did not.

At Karoly's home, Clement asked Daniels a number of questions which indicated he was well aware of the secret training received by British agents. Barratt posed questions as well.[18]

Clement, who had been Daniels' assigned contact to bring him to the Schandl villa, was not convinced he was the British agent their group had been expecting ...[19]

On November 23, 1944, the still imprisoned British agent Joel Palgi was ordered into a train. It was a convoy headed for a concentration camp. [20]

Meanwhile, Daniels "got acquainted" with Karoly Schandl and his contacts, failing to mention that he was a pro-Stalinist underground member of the Communist party.

Notes:

1. Istvan Szent-Miklosy, *With the Hungarian Independence Movement 1943-1947* (Praeger Publishers 1988)
2. C. Schandl, *Sword of the Turul* (Lulu Press 2005)
3. i. HS 4/129
   ii. C. Schandl, *Sword of the Turul* (Lulu Press 2005)
4. HS 9/461/7
5. H. Senesh, *Hannah Senesh: Her Life and Diary, the First complete Edition* (Jewish Lights Publishing 2004) *p 306*
6. i. HS 9/461/7
   ii. HS 4/246
7. WO 208/3405 *(MI9 personnel file of Nussbacher (Palgi), with reports)*
8. HS 4/246
9. Alex Weissberg, *Desperate Mission: Joel Brand's Story* (Criterion Books 1958)
10. Ibid
11. Ibid
12. Ibid
13. WO 208/3405 *(MI9 personnel file of Nussbacher (Palgi), with reports)*
14. HS 4/129
15. Ibid
16. Ibid
17. Ibid
18. i. HS 9/461/7
    ii. HS 4/246
19. Ibid
20. WO 208/3405 *(MI9 personnel file of Nussbacher (Palgi), with reports)*

CHAPTER 12
JOEL PALGI'S ESCAPE

Joel Palgi's train was headed for Germany. He knew he stood little chance of survival once they arrived, So he wasted no time in putting his training to use. [1]

With a few other men, Palgi succeeded in breaking the side of the wagon and jumped off the train. [2]

He returned to Budapest on foot. [3]

Back in the city a free man, he immediately went to the French Legation for assistance. Captain Roose provided him with an address (and a password), where he was certain to find help. [4]

The address was that of the villa of Dr. Antal, the same villa which was administered by Charles Szladits and Raphael Rupert. It was where Reginald Barratt, the man of many aliases, and who was commonly known as TIM, was hiding with a group of POWs.

By then it was around November 30, 1944.

When Palgi arrived at the villa, he was welcomed by TIM, a British RAF flying Officer. [5]

"At that time," Palgi stated, "we did not ask further names." [6]

Tim and Palgi spoke at length. The Englishman was getting ready to go north of Budapest with the other POWs, to hide at the estate of a Hungarian Officer called RAFI, where shelter had been prepared for them. (not to be confused with the "Rafi" whom Palgi later met up with in the Jewish Underground). [7]

86

Hungarian Officer RAFI was likely Hungarian Officer Raphael Rupert, who had already prepared the family estate for the POWs

Tim provided Palgi with forged documents and helped him get in touch with the Zionist Underground Movement for Youth. Palgi then remained in the Swiss Legation, the center of the resistance movement of Zionist youth. He was "in cognito" and was active in rescuing Jews until the Russian occupation. [8]

Palgi managed to elude the NKVD until the British Military Mission opened in Budapest, in late April. He spent some time in Bucharest and helped arrange for Hannah Senesh's mother to be transported to Palestine. Tragically, he also learned that his parents and his sister had been among the casualties of the concentration camps. [9]

Joel Palgi left Hungary for good on June 21, 1945, when he was flown to Bari on a C-47 aircraft. [10]

Notes

1. WO 208/3405 *(MI9 personnel file of Nussbacher (Palgi), with reports)*
2. Ibid
3. Ibid
4. Ibid
5. Ibid
6. Ibid
7. Ibid
8. Ibid
9. Ibid
10. Ibid

CHAPTER 13
ALLIED ORDERS

By the end of November 1944, everyone knew that an Allied victory was imminent. The British in Bari, however, still requested the monthly reports to the Center – the reports that Gabor and his friends were supposed to provide.[1]

It is not known whether any of those reports survived or whether they too fell victim to the curious disappearance of certain documents following the war. However, one thing is certain – the Tito partisans to whom the reports were passed did indeed deliver them to the Allies in Bari. If they hadn't, Gabor Haraszty (ALBERT) would have learned of it during his visit to Bari in the summer of 1944.

As Schandl later wrote in his memoirs (see *Sword of the Turul, 2005*), the reason the reports to the Center were to now be delivered via the Russians instead of the Tito partisans whose route had been blocked, was simple. The British had ordered it.[2]

A Jewish Palestinian sergeant had been sent ahead. He hadn't gotten through.[3]

Gabor then asked Karoly to accept the task.[4]

Karoly was initially apprehensive.

He told a confidant.

"They want me to go to the Russian front."

The confidant had a dire warning. "Don't go to the Russian front, my friend. If you go, we will never see you again."

But Karoly had already agreed to go. He was not going to let his friend down. The British had ordered the delivery of the report via the Russians, so the group had no choice. And considering that Karoly was their best navigator, they knew he would succeed.[5]

The timing was ideal. His unit from Hungarian anti-Aircraft Headquarters would be relocated elsewhere in a few days.

The group soon decided that it would be most advisable for Karoly to cross the Russian lines with a courier – someone who could be verified as a British agent. After all, a Hungarian showing up with a message for the Russians on the front lines was bound to arouse their suspicions.

The courier was Dutch Lieutenant Gerit Van der Waals. The fair haired Van der Waals had played a key role in the British-Dutch Underground for years, and spoke excellent German.

Karoly informed his parents that he would soon be leaving.

His father wanted to know the details.

Karoly informed them he had to take a British agent across the Russian front. He would later return, he promised, and at the time, he believed it.

Shortly before his departure, Clement and Barratt came to Karoly's home for a clandestine meeting in his apartment. They spoke with Karoly in the presence of his friend Kari, as well as the British agent "Daniels".[6]

They were aware of the fact that Karoly was to proceed with a courier.

Both Clement and Barratt stated that they too intended to report to the Russians … within days.[7]

It was the last time Karoly would see Reginald Barratt.

He would eventually see Clement again – but it would be in a Soviet prison.

December 4, 1944

December 1944 had begun as a cold month, as if warning of things to come. On December 4, 1944, Karoly Schandl set out from Budapest with Gerit Van der Waals. [8]

Gerit Van der Waals had been active in the underground. for years. He had been the first Dutch Officer to arrive in Hungary. He had introduced Colonel Howie to Smit - the Director of Philips radio in the Balkans - and he was an expert in making false documents. As Van der Waals informed Schandl, Swedish diplomat Raoul Wallenberg paid him for his services every month. Schandl was not surprised. He already knew Van der Waals was among the best producers of false ID's in Budapest. [9]

THE MISSION

The mission was risky, though not impossible.

The report to the Center was expected by the British, who had ordered it delivered via the Russians instead of the Tito partisans, as the route to the Tito partisans was no longer directly accessible. The information was concealed in a pocket flashlight carried by Karoly Schandl.

The Palestinian sergeant who had originally been sent to deliver the same report had not arrived. He had been sent by Lieutenant Haraszty. [10]

Gabor had then arranged for Gerit Van der Waals to accompany Karoly because he was a British courier and a British agent. The British were Allies of the Russians. Van der Waals' presence was key, for although Karoly had been actively helping British intelligence, he was still a Lieutenant in the Hungarian army. It would have been tantamount to suicidal for him to carry out this mission alone, particularly as they were crossing the Russian front.

It had all been pre-arranged. The Russians would forward Van der Waals to the British Intelligence Service, he would pass on the report in Bari, and the British would then help him reach the Dutch. Meanwhile, Karoly would be forwarded to the alleged newly formed anti-Nazi Hungarian government. [11]

ORDER TO REPORT

The need to pass on the requested report was understandable. But why was Karoly so abruptly leaving Budapest? For that matter, why were Clement and Barratt discussing that they themselves would report to the Russians around the same time as Karoly? In addition, Gabor Haraszty had promised his friends that as soon as the Russians arrived in Budapest, he would put on his British uniform and report to the Russian Commander, to ask for food and supplies for the escapees in hiding. [12] This had obviously been his order – and the order for the men in his group was that they should leave Budapest at once.

Gabor Haraszty must have learned that he was a marked man.

Chances were high that Gabor had discovered the truth from Joel Palgi, after Palgi had escaped. Once in Budapest, Joel had made his way to the French Embassy, which had led him to the very same villa where Reginald Barratt was hiding.

Joel Palgi was welcomed into the villa by "Tim," the RAF airman, who interrogated him. He also met Van der Waals. [13]

"Tim" knew Palgi was one of the Jewish parachutists. Palgi was moved by Tim's commitment to helping and saving as many among the persecuted Jewish population as possible. They spoke at length and shortly afterwards, Tim arranged for Van der Waals to take Palgi to the Zionist Underground. [14]

Joel Palgi was an excellent intelligence agent. It was not a coincidence that he ended up at the villa of Reginald

Barratt, who was ALBERT's close and trusted helper, and that it was the same villa which was overseen by Charles Szladits, whose name ALBERT had given to Bari as a useful helper. Even if it was a coincidence, it would not have taken him long to realize it.

Many were aware of the fact that Reginald Barratt - the man of many aliases - was actively involved in a group led by British intelligence. ALBERT's group. Palgi had likely passed the message on to Barratt that the Gestapo and Hungarian counter-intelligence were aware of the existence of the British agent ALBERT and they had been actively searching for him. The situation was doubly dangerous for Gabor Haraszty (ALBERT), for he was not only a British Lieutenant, but also of Jewish origin.

Even if he had never met ALBERT personally, documents indicate Palgi was indeed aware that ALBERT was in Budapest and that he had friendly contact with the Zionists in Yugoslavia, including Reuven Dafni (GARY).

ALBERT had also met and prepared a report for Palgi's superior, Lawson - in Bari - and had things gone according to plan, ALBERT operations and the Zionists' CHICKEN operations would have worked together.

The enemy was still unaware of ALBERT's actual identity, but it was only a matter of time. Either the Nazis or the Arrow Cross would locate ALBERT – or an informer would lead them to him.

Gabor must have reacted swiftly upon hearing the news. As the siege of Budapest had not yet begun, he was still in contact with Bari. He would have communicated the news that ALBERT was known to the Germans. He would have communicated this to the Allies and awaited further instructions. Too many lives hung in the balance.

Upon learning the enemy was seeking the British agent

ALBERT, his British superiors must have given an order for his group

Report to the Russians as soon as possible.
They were instructed to identify themselves to the Russians as part of ALBERT's group.

Gabor too was to report to the Russians – as soon as they arrived in Budapest. And he was instructed to put on his uniform and report to the Russian Commander after the Russians had arrived. [15]

Shortly before Palgi had crossed into Hungary from Yugoslavia, Major Eden had advised agents to wear their British uniforms – a notion Palgi rejected as it would have proven too risky. [16] *It was, however, obviously protocol for a British Officer to identify himself as such by donning his uniform. Hence, it may be concluded that it was not Gabor Haraszty's idea that he should present himself to the Russians in British uniform. It had been an order from the British.*

RENDEZVOUS

When Karoly Schandl left his home at 16-18 Kelenhegyi Street, he had no idea he would never return. He had no idea he would never see his good friend Gabor again. He also had no idea that Gerit Van der Waals would be transported east, along with him. [17]

The only thing he knew at the time was the British had given him orders to carry out, and although those orders were extremely high risk, he was the one who would get through to have the last report delivered. Of that he was certain. [18]

They arrived at the designated meeting place on foot, without incident. It was the estate of a family friend, south of Lake Velence. Once there, Karoly and Van der Waals waited for the Russians to arrive. [19]

When they did, it was not the reception the two men had anticipated. They were roughly apprehended and accused of being German spies, as a pretext. [20]

Karoly and Van der Waals repeated to their NKVD captors that ALBERT had sent them. [21]

The Russians were not interested, despite the fact that the meeting had been prearranged through the British. Furthermore, they showed no interest in any information Karoly and the young Dutchman might have been able to provide.

They refused to forward the two men anywhere.

The NKVD and SMERSH men were angry. They repeatedly accused Schandl and Van der Waals of being spies.[22]

First they accused them of being German spies.

They then demanded to know why they had been helping the British and the Americans instead of the Russians.

Karoly replied that he had not met any Russians in Budapest.

He repeated that ALBERT had sent them.

They did not seem to be listening.

In fact, they behaved in an openly hostile manner.

The separate interrogations of Karoly and the Dutch Lieutenant went on for a few days. [23]

Things then started to happen fast, in a very interesting sequence ...

On December 7, 1944, the last Kasztner train of Jewish escapees arrived in Switzerland *(Kasztner had gotten out of Hungary and had been in Switzerland since the end of November).* [24]

On December 8, 1944, the Soviets officially arrested Karoly Schandl, who had been working for British agent ALBERT. [25]

On December 8, 1944, the Soviets officially arrested Gerit Van der Waals, who had been working as a courier for British agent ALBERT.

On December 8, 1944, the Soviets officially arrested RAF Officer Reginald Barratt, who had been helping British agent ALBERT. [26]

On December 8, 1944, Raoul Wallenberg wrote letters from Budapest to his family - for the last time.[27]

Notes:

1. C. Schandl, *Sword of the Turul* (Lulu Press 2005)
2. Ibid
3. Ibid
4. Ibid
5. Ibid
6. HS 9/461/7
7. Ibid
8. C. Schandl, *Sword of the Turul* (Lulu Press 2005)
9. Ibid
10. Ibid
11. Ibid
12. Ibid
13. WO 208/3405 *(MI9 personnel file of Nussbacher (Palgi), with reports)*
14. Ibid
15. C. Schandl, *Sword of the Turul* (Lulu Press 2005)
16. Y. Palgi, *Into the Inferno: the Memoir of a Jewish Paratrooper Behind Nazi Lines* (Rutgers University Press 2003)
17. C. Schandl, *Sword of the Turul* (Lulu Press 2005)
18. Ibid
19. Ibid
20. Ibid
21. Ibid
22. Ibid
23. Ibid
24. Kasztner Memorial Site
25. C. Schandl, *Sword of the Turul* (Lulu Press 2005)
26. Raphael Rupert, *Red Wire and the Lubianka* (Ballinakella 1991)
27. Raoul Wallenberg, *Letters and Dispatches 1924-1944* (Arcade Publishing 1996)

CHAPTER 14
THE SENIOR DUTCH OFFICER

LIEUTENANT VAN HOOTEGEM

Edward Van Hootegem was the senior Officer of the Dutch in Hungary. The Dutch were known as master forgers who also excelled in organizing prisoners' escapes. As Hungary considered itself neutral toward the Dutch, they had been protected. In fact, until the arrival of the Germans, the Dutch had been able to move about quite openly. [1]

Following the German occupation of March 1944, Van Hootegem had remained in contact with Colonel Howie. [2]

Howie, as the official head of the Allied POWs in Hungary, had appointed New Zealander Captain Roy Natusch as commander of the POWs when they had been staying at Count Andrassy's castle in the town of Szigetvar. [3]

After his daring escape from the Gestapo at Szigetvar, Roy Natusch located Reginald Barratt, who had also avoided capture by the Gestapo. Barratt had found refuge at the home of a friend in Szigetvar. Together, Natusch and Barratt made their way to Budapest. Barratt knew passable Hungarian and was able to read the train schedule. [4]

Once in Budapest, they approached the Revered Szent-Ivanyi, who was, at that time, unable to provide lodging at his church, as he believed the Germans were watching him. He advised them to go to the flat of Evelyn Gore Symes, the secretary of a neutral legation. Through Gore Symes, Natusch was put in touch with Frank Brackel, a tall, red-haired Dutch

Officer who was a friend of Van Hootegem. [5]

As Howie had spoken highly of Van Hootegem, Natusch knew he was reliable. [6]

Brackel took Natusch to Van Hootegem, who agreed to arrange a meeting between Natusch and the now elusive Colonel Howie, with whom Natusch had lost contact. [7]

They met on a quiet street in the Zugliget area at night. Howie's hat was pulled down to partially conceal his face. He advised Natusch to leave Hungary, as the Gestapo knew who Natusch was. [7]

Howie, at that time, had decided to stay in Hungary, though, as indicated in various documents, he did periodically express an interest in going to Yugoslavia – which was then Natusch's destination.

The Colonel agreed to arrange for two fake passports – which Natusch had planned to use for himself and Reginald Barratt. [8]

Howie told him that the Reverend Szent-Ivanyi would send him a message when the passports were ready. [9]

They shook hands and went their separate ways. Shortly afterwards, as promised, Szent-Ivanyi informed Natusch of two passports that had been left for him at the neutral legation. [10]

Natusch promptly went to the legation to pick up the passports. There he ran into "Tom Sanders." [11]

"Tom Sanders" was the alias of Weinstein, the Jewish Palestinian British soldier who was in fact Hungarian. Weinstein had managed to avoid capture by the Germans in the castle of Szigetvar by hiding in a cupboard until they left. He was in dire straits, as he was Jewish and he had no false papers. [12]

Natusch ended up giving the false passports to Barratt and Weinstein, who then went south together to make contact with the Tito partisans. [13]

Natusch waited for their return but, unfortunately, lost all communication with Weinstein and Barratt. [14]

Barratt and Weinstein later resurfaced with the group of Gabor Haraszty and Karoly Schandl. This is not surprising, as ALBERT's group was part of Dubreuil's network, and Dubreuil of the British Secret Service was working with Howie and Van Hootegem.

Van Hootegem then came to the assistance of Roy Natusch by providing him with a passport which identified him as a Dutchman. He also arranged for him to hide in a Dutch household in Buda. [15]

The capital was increasingly dangerous. High ranking, politically connected collaborators of the anti-Nazi resistance had already been taken away to the Gestapo prison and a group of Polish officers in a house in Buda were massacred by a band of fascists. [16]

In April 1944, Roy Natusch was himself arrested by the Gestapo. He was transported out of Hungary but later, the tough and well-liked Captain escaped and joined up with the Tito partisans. [17]

Van Hootegem and Howie stayed in close contact, working together to help Allied POWs, among other things. However, the South African Colonel also had to flee when the Gestapo were closing in on his party, in September 1944. [18]

The Dutch officers remained and survived the siege of Budapest, though Van Hootegem's group soon ran into their own difficulties. In 1945, they were placed under arrest – by the Red Army ... [19]

Moscow – March 1945

According to a previously Top Secret document in U.K. National Archives files concerning SOE/Soviet/NKVD Relations in Hungary, an unusual meeting took place in Moscow on March 28, 1945. [20]

It was described in a "most secret cipher telegram" sent to the War Office and M.I.3 "for action" - by Brinckman of 30 Military Mission Moscow. [21]

The 30 Military Mission had been sent to Moscow by the British in 1943 and was engaged in brokering the exchange of military intelligence between the "Allies."

Brinckman reported that the Dutch Ambassador had permitted him to interview Dutch Lieutenant E.J.C. Van Hootegem (Royal Guards Hunters), who had been taken to Moscow as per the orders of the Soviet GS. [22]

The reason for Van Hootegem's detainment in Moscow did not appear in the cipher.

Brinckman explained he had been able to elicit information from Van Hootegem despite the fact that he spoke English "badly." [23]

This, however, was an inaccurate assessment of the Dutch Officer's linguistic capability. Roy Natusch, who had communicated in English with Van Hootegem, described him as having spoken near-perfect English. [24]

So why did 30 Military Mission in Moscow convey to the War Office in London that the Dutchman's English was at a low level? Was it to cover up the fact that they were not transmitting all the information he had told them? Or had Van Hootegem himself pretended not to be as fluent as he really was, as he hadn't entirely trusted the 30 Military Mission?

THE DUTCH AND BRITISH UNDERGROUND

Conflicting language assessment aside, Van Hootegem did provide 30 Military Mission with a great deal of information.

He told them that as of March 3, 1944, he had met several times with Louis Clement, Lieutenant-Colonel Howie, Mr. Dubreuil, and Lafayette, all of whom were working for the British Secret Intelligence Service. The group had been passing on to the Allies intelligence about airfields, factories, and oil refineries. The information had been transmitted by means of a short-wave radio set operated by none other than Clement. [25]

Van Hootegem went on to say that during his time in Budapest, the group had also liberated a number of POWs from the Hungarians, who had since been sent to Odessa, Soviet Union. [26]

Some of the POW's names he remembered were ...

Gordon Park (New Zealand)
Archibald Hepburn (Scotland)
William Jones (London)
Reginald Barratt (RAF)
Gordon Tasker

A number of the men, including Reginald Barratt, had been arrested en route to Debrecen and were then taken to Russia. [27]

Van Hootegem also reported that Roy Natusch had been arrested by the Gestapo and taken back to Germany (at the time he was unaware that the resourceful Natusch had once more escaped). [28]

He pointed out that Howie had been flown out of Hungary to Italy in autumn 1944. [29]

When the Russians entered Budapest, they asked Van Hootegem several questions, yet he did not divulge everything to them. Nevertheless, he was accused of working for the British Intelligence Service and subsequently imprisoned – for six weeks. [30]

There were two Hungarians in his guarded cell – and the Russians treated them all as if they were the enemy. [31]

Van Hootegem also described what he had witnessed during the siege of Budapest. The Germans had fought hard against the Red Army, though the Hungarians had not, likely due to the fact that they were pro-Anglo-American. [32]

He had been able to identify the Feldherranhooee Regiment by the red and white squares on their vehicles. The entire regiment was destroyed. [33]

There were thousands of dead Germans in the streets of Budapest. During the earlier stages of the siege, many Russians had been killed. [34]

The Russian POW claims included "all male civilians in the military zone." [35]

The Russian Commander had told the Dutch Officer that due to the murder of Russian armistice delegates - which was true and not a rumor - the city would be forced to endure the worst things imaginable. [36]

The behavior of the Russians included looting, and raping as many as half of the women in Budapest, including Dutch and French girls. [37]

According to the Dutch Officer, the Russians did not seem to make any distinction between the Germans and the Allies. [38]

Van Hootegem had been taken to Moscow with 19 other Dutchmen and 16 Belgians. He noted that included in the group was a member of the SS, whom the Russians were pretending was a Dutchman. The name of the SS man was not given.[39]

The secret cipher telegram to the War Office went on to say that the Russians had placed all of Van Hootegem's party in barracks outside Moscow. [40]

There was also another English-speaking Dutch officer with "interesting information" who was in captivity in Moscow, but it had not been possible for the British to have contact with him. [41]

Lieutenant Van Hootegem had been able to communicate with his captors in Russian. He had continued to deny any involvement in the British Intelligence Service. [42]

Eventually the NKVD must have believed him, for they permitted him to leave Russia via Odessa with some of his men. [43]

It may have been more dramatic than that, however. Some said that a group of Dutch Officers had managed to catch the attention of some British Officers at a train station en route to Moscow before the Dutchmen were transported to their final destination. Once they were spotted by the British, the NKVD had no choice but to release them to the British.

Unfortunately, Gerit Van der Waals had no such luck, nor did Karoly Schandl. Although the British were aware of their imprisonment by 1945, they seemed unable to do anything about it.

Notes:

1. K. Kapronczay *Refugees in Hungary: Shelter from the Storm During World War II* (Matthias Corvinus Publishing 1999)
2. HS 4/103
3. F.S. Jones, *The Double Dutchman* (Corgi Books 1978)
4. Ibid
5. Ibid
6. Ibid
7. Ibid
8. Ibid
9. Ibid
10. Ibid

11. Ibid
12. Ibid
13. Ibid
14. Ibid
15. Ibid
16. Ibid
17. Ibid
18. HS 9/753/2 *(SOE Personnel File of Howie)*
19. HS 4/103
20. Ibid
21. Ibid
22. Ibid
23. Ibid
24. F.S. Jones, *The Double Dutchman* (Corgi Books 1978)
25. HS 4/103
26. Ibid
27. Ibid
28. Ibid
29. Ibid
30. Ibid
31. Ibid
32. Ibid
33. Ibid
34. Ibid
35. Ibid
36. Ibid
37. Ibid
38. Ibid
39. Ibid
40. Ibid
41. Ibid
42. Ibid
43. K. Kapronczay *Refugees in Hungary: Shelter from the Storm During World War II* (Matthias Corvinus Publishing 1999)

CHAPTER 15
THE BRITISH MILITARY MISSION

By January 1945, a dark cloud hung over the agony of the Hungarian capital. The Battle of Budapest was underway. It was a bloody siege, which would claim high casualties among the civilian population, comparable in losses to Stalingrad.

On February 13, 1945, the Illustrated London News reported that Budapest had been liberated.

According to a Swiss legation report prepared in the spring of 1945, half of Budapest had been destroyed. Following the siege, Russian troops had looted, emptied and removed bank safes, raped females from the ages of 10 to 70 years, committed murders, confiscated documents, refused to accept passports issued by the Swiss legation, hindered freedom of movement, and started mass deportations to the east *(J.F. Montgomery, 'Hungary – the Unwilling Satellite' Devin-Adair Company, 1947).*

Budapest – 1945

The British Military Mission had established a presence in the war-torn Hungarian capital by late April 1945.
Shortly thereafter, Joel Palgi was approached by a representative of Rakosi's secretary.[1] Matyas Rakosi, a newly installed communist leader in Hungary, had returned from the Soviet Union with the Red Army to take his place in

the newly planned totalitarian order. A self-described disciple of Stalin, he would later make his mark on history as a murderous dictator who exterminated his political foes in purges similar to those of Joseph Stalin.

When the British Military Mission opened its doors in Budapest in 1945, however, Rakosi's secretary had more clandestine matters in mind. The request to Palgi was simple. They wanted Palgi to watch and report to them the names of all individuals who entered and left the British Mission. In short, they wanted him to spy for the Communist party. [2]

It was evident that Rakosi was already gathering the names of pro-Western Hungarians.

Palgi immediately reported the incident to Captain Bloodworth of the British Military Mission, to warn him - though it is unknown what, if any, precautions were then taken to protect the men and women who passed through the doors of the Mission. [3]

Fortunately for Palgi, following harassment by the NKVD and a few months working for the International Red Cross, he was finally transported by the British to Palestine – and safety. At his own request, he was subsequently discharged from the army. The British commended him on his excellent conduct and service. [4]

Central Europe had indeed lost a hero in Joel Palgi, who went on to do great things in Israel, leading the first unit of parachutists in the War of Independence. He also became the Head of El Al Airlines and served as Israel's Ambassador to Tanzania. [5]

Meanwhile, the situation in Hungary was dire. The correspondence between the British stationed in Budapest and the War Office in London showed that they were aware of night-time killings committed by the occupying Russians, in addition to the censorship that was already imposed on the newspapers. Nevertheless, the British continued to refer to the Russians as "our Allies." [6]

KAROLY SCHANDL SR. AND THE BRITISH

After the siege of Budapest, the "new normal" began to take shape in Hungary and for many there was nowhere to turn, despite certain outward appearances.

As the shell-shocked and desperate people who remained in the destroyed capital attempted to survive, the British Military Mission (BMM) set out to liquidate its agents and their helpers. It was desired to settle these accounts so that the British could leave the Russian occupied land as quickly as possible. A young British officer who had been approved by the Russians was soon appointed to help with the task. He was already known to a number of Hungarians. [7]

He himself had been present in the capital prior to and during the siege, and had had contact with some of the key players in this book.

Though official contact with Hungarians was no longer permitted, the Hungarians who had become British agents and helpers were approached and interviewed by the British during this time. There were also a number of visitors to the Mission, many of whom had assisted the Allies and were now themselves in need of assistance. [8]

One such visitor to the BMM in the summer of 1945 was Karoly Schandl Sr., a man the young British officer recognized immediately. [9]

The impeccably dressed former statesman sat solemnly in the chair across from the officer and came straight to the point.

"I am here about my son."

The officer replied that he knew his son and was well aware of how much he had done for Daniels. [10]

Mr. Schandl, however, was not there to discuss Daniels, who had left with the Russians in February without any problems.

"My son has not returned."

The officer waited for him to continue.

He did.

"He was to take a British agent across the front lines to

the Russians. The Russians were to forward the agent to the British Intelligence Service and my son to the newly formed anti-Nazi Hungarian government."

"This was during the siege?"

"No, it was just before the siege. He left with the British agent on December 4. They were to cross the lines just south of Lake Velence."

Mr. Schandl stared at the Officer in a very intense manner and waited for his reply.

The officer assured him he would look into the matter and do all he could to help the family, as he knew how much they had done for Daniels. [11]

Mr. Schandl nodded, stood up, and took his leave from the British Military Mission. There was no more to say, except to wait for the results of the inquiry. He had ventured to the British to inform them of the matter, as his son had been actively involved with British intelligence, and he was confident the meeting would yield results. They would certainly be able to locate him.

He returned home to the damaged family villa and told his wife about the meeting. Terezia had been sick with worry. Not all of Karoly Jr.'s friends could be accounted for.

TOP SECRET COMMUNICATIONS

The Schandl Case

What transpired next, however, was a bizarre exchange of cipher telegrams between the BMM, the War Office, and the Inter-Service Liaison Department. In a top secret and personal message to the War Office in London, Lt-Col. Boughey was informed that Schandl had passed through the lines with an unidentified British officer during the siege, and then vanished. It was then stated that an unidentified Hungarian lieutenant who was also believed to be an ISLD agent reported that Schandl had shown up in Turkey. As

Schandl himself was known to be involved with ISLD, it was assumed that he had reported upon arrival in Turkey. The War Office was asked to look into whether Schandl had reported in Istanbul. [12]

A few weeks later, the War Office responded that they were working on the query regarding Schandl's whereabouts. and would soon "revert." The next cipher indicated that ISLD in Istanbul had been contacted as to whether Schandl had arrived. By the end of August, the representative in Istanbul reported that there was no news at all of Schandl having shown up in Turkey. One of ISLD's agents who had previously worked in Budapest, however, was able to provide the following information. Schandl had passed through the lines with an agent who was acting as a British courier. The courier was known to have been arrested by the Russians, after which time no news was heard of him. The conclusion was that Schandl had likely met with the same fate. Further communication was promised if more definite news was received, but that was pretty much the end of the matter. [13a]

Meanwhile, Dr. Schandl Sr. was contacted with talk of a medal and compensation for having been such a trusted contact of the British during the war, though he was not interested in any such things, nor was he willing to sign any document they put before him, agreeing to absolve the British government of any future responsibility. And why would he have signed? His son had been on a mission arranged by the British – and no one would tell the Schandls what had become of him. [13b]

Excerpt from HS 4/129

<u>TOP SECRET AND PERSONAL</u>
BRITISH MILITARY MISSION HUNGARY
BUDAPEST

24th July, 1945

The son of Charles Schandl (Daniels' protector) who went through the lines with an unknown British Officer during the siege and disappeared is now believed to have turned up in Turkey. Christian name is also Charles. Source is thought to be a Hungarian Lieutenant possibly employed by I.S.L.D. Would you ask Istanbul whether he has reported and if so solicit news? The young man helped (Daniels) a good deal whilst he was in hiding …

Lt-Col Peter BOUGHEY,
M.O.1 (S.P.)
The War Office,
LONDON. S.W.1.

Excerpt from HS 4/129

FROM: WAR OFFICE

TO: ALLIED CONTROL COMMISSION HUNGARY
       (BRITISH DELEGATION)

IMPORTANT

69426 CIPHER C.A.6.   AUG. 45.

TOP SECRET

WE HAVE NO RECORD SUCH PARTY. AM ASKING MI6. WILL REVERT.

Excerpt from HS 4/129

M.O.1. (S.P.)
THE WAR OFFICE
S.W.1.

QIK/HU/8O6

29th August, 1945

… As we no longer have a post in Turkey, we have been in touch with I.S.L.D., who are enquiring in Istanbul as to whether Charles SCHANDL has arrived. When we hear from them I will inform you.

Excerpt from HS 4/129

JMC/1043

To: A/CD 31. 8.45

From: A.C.S.S.

Your ACD/179/8042 of 24th August

We are trying to obtain from our representative in Istanbul any information about Schandl having arrived there. So far we have no news.

2. We have heard from an agent of ours who was previously working in Budapest that Schandl passed through the lines with another agent who was acting as our courier. This latter individual was arrested by the Russians and we have had no news of him since. It is possible therefore that Schandl may have met with the same fate.

3. I shall let you know if we get more definite news.

Note:
The "agent who was acting as our courier" was a reference to Dutch Lieutenant Gerit Van der Waals.

ALLIED HELPERS

After the 1945 Russian occupation of Hungary, it was not advantageous to have been any kind of helper of the British.

Mrs. Kress, who had hidden Colonel Howie in her flat on Vaci Street during the most dangerous times in Budapest, was herself experiencing problems - at the hands of the Russian occupiers, who were preoccupied with finding out every detail of Howie's activities in Hungary. They accused her of being a German spy as an excuse to detain her, then proceeded with a brutal interrogation. Mrs. Kress was threatened, beaten with rubber truncheons, and forced to sign a confession. Still, she refused to talk about Colonel Howie.[14]

The Polish Countess Tarnopolska, who had worked closely with Howie during his Hungarian stay and was his confidant, was also a person of interest. The Russians tricked her into handing over to them a letter Howie had written, summarizing his activities in Budapest. A Soviet agent had approached her, convinced her he was British and that Howie had requested she pass on his letter to him. Evidently the NKVD had already been aware of the letter's existence.[15]

The Countess, who found refuge in the hostel of the Reverend Szent-Ivanyi, married an older Englishman, at which time she became Mrs. Meeson and set about making arrangements to leave for England. Though she was later recommended for a King's Medal for courage, the War Office was quick to point out that the King's Medal for courage was only awarded to foreigners, hence Mrs. Meeson was no longer eligible. Mrs. Meeson's newly acquired British citizenship enabled her to leave Hungary in August 1945.[16]

A number of helpers and collaborators of the British in Hungary were known to have been carted off by the Russians, while others experienced problems after giving statements to the representative of the British Military Mission. The Mission found itself in a precarious, albeit contradictory position. On the one hand, official contacts with Hungarians were not permitted, yet on the other, Hungarian helpers and collaborators of the British were approached for interviews, after which time they were offered a letter of thanks from His Majesty and, in certain cases, some form of compensation. [17]

Within the BMM, there also seemed to be an underlying atmosphere of discord. Certain officers complained of the bureaucracy, a lack of funds, and the inability to even so much as send a cipher telegram without first having it approved through a lengthy chain of command. Nevertheless, they were not above breaking the rules, such as secretly hiring an outsider to help run errands. An outsider who was not anti-Russian, and was paid from the pocket of his British employer, who boasted in a top secret and personal handwritten letter to his friend at the War Office that the Mission would surely object had they known he had secretly hired this individual (whose name has been removed in the released records of the National Archives). [18]

There was also an interesting bit of correspondence written by the same British officer, requesting that his contact at the War Office help him obtain copies of personal letters Colonel Howie had written, though his reasons were not given. The officer further complained that he had been unable to see the private letter which Howie had written to the Brigadier at the BMM. [19]

Some letters received by the British mirrored the sheer desperation of Hungarians who had reportedly been promised British Nationality while helping the Allies, only to find that the promise would not be upheld once the war was over. [20]

Some Hungarians who made it to the West in later years had criticism of the "help" which was provided by the Mission. It was said that if one informed the British in Budapest of an Allied prisoner being held by the Soviets, the BMM might inform the Soviets first, rather than the British higher command. As a result, the Soviets had ample time to move the prisoner in question - after which time they invited the British to come and see for themselves that there was no such prisoner …

This was rumored to have been the case with RAF Officer Reginald Barratt.

SOE AGENT CLEMENT (KLEMENT)

When one of the lists of agents in Hungary had been compiled by the British, the name Lajos (Lewis/Louis, a.k.a. Tibor) Clement showed up. It was claimed that he had last been heard of in 1941 and was paid 8000 pengoes regarding sabotage he had undertaken on behalf of the Allies. [21]

Clement, however, had been visible just prior to the siege. He had, in fact, been seen by another British agent at Karoly Schandl's home – in late 1944 – not to mention that agents of the British Secret Service (including Dubreuil) had used him as a radio operator throughout 1944, to transmit intelligence to the Allies. Some of that intelligence had been gathered by Gabor Haraszty (ALBERT) and his friends, so it was no surprise that Clement had also been in direct contact with Karoly Schandl.

Clement had a confidant in L. Csuros, a helpful Hungarian engineer in Budapest who had repaired "United Nations" radios for the Allies. Csuros often kept in his flat broadcasting equipment for the underground. In addition, he had helped to obtain useful military forms and rubber stamps which were of great assistance in the forging of papers. Csuros had not only been a confidant of Clement, but had further helped him by hiding his radio in his house – a radio which some British officers had also referred to as the "Polish set." [22]

It was no surprise that the radio was referred to as the Polish set, for as late as 1944, Clement had been sending messages to the British Secret Intelligence Service via the Hungarian-based network of Jacques Dubreuil, who was both a British agent and a Polish national.

Thus, the early claim that someone among the ranks of the British made - that Clement had not been heard of since 1941 - was completely inaccurate. He had been in direct contact with British agents and the Allies for three years after that time.

But what had become of Clement after December 1944 …?

On July 21, 1945, M.W.V. Maude of the Foreign Office wrote to H.N. Sporborg, Esq., C.M.C. that he had received news of a genuine British agent who was being held at a Russian prison camp.[23]

This information had been passed on to the Foreign Office by a Dutch Lieutenant – Harteveld – who had himself been imprisoned by the Russians, along with Dutch and other Allied prisoners in February 1945. The Russians had accused them of being secret British agents and put them through very tough interrogations.[24]

Harteveld also passed on the name of the genuine British agent to the Foreign Office. He was Louis Clement, and he had been a known prisoner of the Russians in April 1945.[25]

Sporborg's reply to the Foreign Office was that Clement was indeed one of the agents of the Special Operations Executive (SOE). The British Military Mission in Budapest brought up the matter of his release in late summer of 1945 with Russian Marshal Voroshilov. Some in the ranks of the British were extremely concerned as they'd heard Clement was having a hard time of it. Others had a less urgent approach to the matter, breezily stating that it was up to their Allies (i.e. the Russians) to decide his fate, so there was nothing to do but wait.[26]

The BMM communication with Voroshilov did not yield results. It was then suggested that P.W.5 in London should take up Clement's release with the Soviet Embassy there.[27]

In addition, the appropriate persons at the War Office were contacted concerning a request that the Foreign Office should have H.M. Ambassador in Moscow take the matter to a high level with the Russians in Moscow. [28]

Around the same time, an officer at the British Military Mission passed on to his superiors the (Clement) Vajda Report, an account of Clement's early contact with the Ambassador to Madrid. It concerned a W/T set which Clement had been scheduled to pick up from an apartment in the Budapest Royal Palace. It pertained to what the Officer called the "Pejacsevich line" and was connected to Operation Pilatus. *In this case, Clement was reported to have "worked well in the absence of a courier."* [29]

Both the War Office and the Foreign Office became involved in the case of the captured Clement, and there were high level negotiations at the London-Moscow level. [30] Nevertheless, no channels proved successful and thus he too was doomed to become a long term "guest" of the Soviets.

And yet, for some strange reason, his name (and corresponding serial number) presently shows up on a Military Memorial in the U.K., his date of death incorrectly given as 1943. [31]

Excerpt from HS 4/129

DRAFT

From: H.M. Sporborg, Esq., C.M.G.

To: Mr. M.W.V. Maude
  The Foreign Office

Lieut. Clement, whom you mentioned, is an agent of ours, who was in Hungary and who is now in the hands of the Russians. B.M.M., Hungary have taken up the matter of his release with Marshal Voroshilov and suggest that it should be taken even higher as their approach has elicited no action on the part of the Russians. We understand that P.W.5. in London are about to take up the matter with the Soviet Embassy here.[32]

Clement's File

According to his file, Clement (Klement) was a Hungarian who had joined the French Foreign Legion at a young age. He was later trained as a parachutist by the Free French forces after recovering from an injury in Scotland. He then was reported to have been interned on the Isle of Man and also worked as a theatre stage hand in London. [33]

Shortly afterwards, he was said to have joined the British Special Operations Executive, and began his training in 1942. [34]

However, according to a 1945 report of the SOE in Hungary, Clement had already been paid to undertake acts of sabotage on behalf of the Allies as early as 1941 and that payment had been in Hungarian pengoes. [35]

A known visitor to Schandl's Budapest home, Tibor Clement/Klement, a.k.a Lewis/Louis/Lajos Clement/Vajda was arrested by the Russians in Hungary in early 1945.

Notes:

1. WO 208/3405 *(MI9 personnel file of Nussbacher (Palgi), with reports)*
2. Ibid
3. Ibid
4. Ibid
5. Y. Palgi, *Into the Inferno: the Memoir of a Jewish Paratrooper Behind Nazi Lines* (Rutgers University Press 2003)

6. HS 4/129
7. Ibid
8. Ibid
9. Ibid
10. Ibid
11. Ibid
12. Ibid
13a. Ibid
13b Ibid
14. Ibid
15. Ibid
16. Ibid
17. Ibid
18. Ibid
19. Ibid
20. Ibid
21. Ibid
22. Ibid
23. Ibid
24. Ibid
25. Ibid
26. Ibid
27. Ibid
28. Ibid
29. Ibid
30. Ibid
31. *Commonwealth War Graves Commission, Brockwood Memorial, Lieutenant L. Klement, Special Operations Executive*
32. HS 4/129
33. HS 9/846 (Klement, Lajos/Louis/Tibor)
34. Ibid
35. HS 4/129

CHAPTER 16
LIQUIDATION

LIQUIDATED

A number of people in contact with the British Underground in Hungary, including the Reverend Szent Ivanyi, heard that Reginald Barratt and Weinstein had been taken away by the Soviets.

What was Weinstein's exact role?

As a British Palestinian sergeant, Weinstein had had contact with both the British and Zionist Underground. As Joel Brand later reported, Weinstein was one of the first escaped British soldiers in Hungary to get in touch with the Jewish Aid and Rescue Committee. After his arrival, Weinstein made contact with Otto Komoly, a Hungarian Zionist leader and the chairman of the Committee.[1]

Komoly worked hard assisting those in need. He was regularly in touch with officials and church leaders. He had also helped organize the rescue train. *Tragically, Komoly was later abducted and murdered by the Arrow Cross.*

Weinstein had also introduced Joel Brand to Colonel Howie, at Howie's request.[2]

According to one written account of Van der Waals' fate, Weinstein had been the Palestinian sergeant who had not made it through, after being sent to the Russian front with a report prior to Van der Waals' attempt. Thus, it was concluded that he had been captured.[3] This would make Weinstein the same Palestinian sergeant whom Gabor Haraszty had sent ahead, before asking Karoly Schandl to take Van der Waals in early December 1944.[4] That would mean Weinstein had been actively involved in ALBERT's group, and the Russians had apprehended him.

Barratt had also been involved with ALBERT's group. He and Clement had visited Karoly Schandl's home in late 1944 to question the newly arrived British agent the group had sprung from prison. The group that was led by ALBERT. The RAF Officer had been aware of the plan to send Schandl and Van der Waals, the courier, across Russian lines. Barratt and Clement also mentioned - in the presence of the British agent in the Schandl villa - their own intention to soon go to the Russians.[5]

Raphael Rupert, who had been a helper of the British, and had provided refuge for Reginald Barratt, would later hear that Barratt had been shot and killed by the Russians in June 1945, having been accused of being a British spy. Rupert himself was later taken to a Soviet gulag, where he spent a number of years.[6]

In early 1945, it was known by the British that Karoly Schandl and Gerit Van der Waals had been secretly transported to prison in Moscow, under heavily armed guard.[7]

By 1945, Gabor Haraszty - code name ALBERT - had himself been arrested by the Russians. He never returned and it was later reported that, tragically, he had not survived his treatment at the hands of the NKVD.[8]

He was reportedly shot.

Raoul Wallenberg, for whom Van der Waals had been working, also vanished from Budapest without a trace. According to a British brigadier general, the Russians had abducted him, despite their claims to the contrary.[9]

THE "SZALAY GROUP"

According to documents in the U.K. National Archives, the "Szalay Group" was a group of Hungarians and Dutch Officers who operated a secret printing press for false papers - and helped the Allied cause. Lieutenant Puckel of the Royal Dutch Army was involved in this group, as were Raphael Rupert - and Clement. [10]

Puckel, the Dutch Officer, was a close friend of Gerit Van der Waals. [11] Since September 1944, Van der Waals had been staying at the Geological Institute, courtesy of Tibor Szalay. [12]

Weinstein himself had been hiding at the institute from September until November 28. [13]

In December 1944, Clement had also found refuge there for 10 days. [14]

These dates provide a great deal of information.

Weinstein was confirmed to have been in hiding in Budapest until November 28. Therefore, he had left the capital and headed south to deliver the report of Haraszty's group only a week before Van der Waals. This means that the British-led group had already learned by early December that Weinstein had not gotten through with the report. This information was received by Bari, as they had been expecting the report. Bari could only have contacted the group by radio – and they evidently did, to notify them that Weinstein had not arrived This indicates that Gabor Haraszty still had radio contact with Bari in early December 1944, just as Karoly Schandl stated in his memoirs.

"The order had come from Bari ..."

The next courier was to be Gerit Van der Waals, the young Dutch Officer who had taken the photographs of Kari and Daniels at Karoly Schandl's home, for their fake IDs. Karoly was to accompany him across the front. [15]

The fact that Clement was reported to have stayed at the Geological Institute for 10 days in December indicates that he did not go to the Russians with Reginald Barratt, who had already been arrested by December 8, 1944. Clement had gone later, though the details of exactly when, where, and with whom he first encountered the Russians remain unknown.

What is known is, that had it not been for a Dutch officer contacting the War Office later in 1945, the real fate of Clement might never have been known. [16]

THE CAVE CHURCH (Sziklatemplom)

The Cave Church near Karoly Schandl's home was well known to the British as having helped the anti-Nazi resistance during the Second World War.

Documents in the U.K. National Archives indicate it was known that "Daniels" the British agent was passed through there and given a disguise as a Paulist monk before being taken to Karoly Schandl's apartment. [17]

In addition, a certain "Brother Kazmer" was listed as a helper of the British, who referred to him as a Polish "cut-out" courier. [18] The fact that Karoly's group was working with the Polish Underground was mentioned by Schandl in his memoirs. This is not surprising, as "Jack," (a.k.a. Jacques Dubreuil), who had gotten his old friends involved in the resistance, was himself Polish.[19]

Brother Kazmer, the "Polish cut-out" was known to have been a frequent visitor to the Schandl villa. [20]

It would have been known by the British that the church had been providing monk's robes to members of Karoly Schandl's resistance group. It would also have been known that due to an "arrangement" with the church, Karoly Schandl's private apartment was designated as a place where convalescing and out of town fathers and brothers could stay. That way, Kari and Daniels were able to move about in their disguises as monks without arousing much suspicion. [21]

In 1951, the church was stormed and sealed by the communists. A number of the fathers and monks were imprisoned.

The head of the Paulist Order, Father Vezer, was hung.

This had all been executed by the Hungarian Communist Secret Police (AVO/AVH), who received their orders from Moscow.

It is not clear how much information about the church and its involvement in the resistance had been shared by the British with their wartime "Allies" – the Russians.

Notes:

1. Alex Weissberg, *Desperate Mission: Joel Brand's Story* (Criterion Books 1958)
2. Ibid
3. K. Kapronczay *Refugees in Hungary: Shelter from the Storm During World War II* (Matthias Corvinus Publishing 1999)
4. C. Schandl, *Sword of the Turul* (Lulu Press 2005)
5. i. HS 9/461/7
   ii. HS 4/246
6. Raphael Rupert, *Red Wire and the Lubianka* (Ballinakella 1991)
7. C. Schandl, *Sword of the Turul* (Lulu Press 2005)
8. Ibid
9. Y. Palgi, *Into the Inferno: the Memoir of a Jewish Paratrooper Behind Nazi Lines* (Rutgers University Press 2003)
10. HS 4/129
11. K. Kapronczay *Refugees in Hungary: Shelter from the Storm During World War II* (Matthias Corvinus Publishing 1999)
12. HS 4/129
13. Ibid
14. Ibid
15. C. Schandl, *Sword of the Turul* (Lulu Press 2005)
16. HS 4/129
17. i. HS 9/461/7
    ii. HS 4/246
18. HS 4/129
19. C. Schandl, *Sword of the Turul* (Lulu Press 2005)
20. i. HS 9/461/7
    ii. HS 4/246
21. C. Schandl, *Sword of the Turul* (Lulu Press 2005)

CHAPTER 17
TOP SECRET

In July 1945, Lieutenant-Colonel A.C. Simonds of MI9 sent a top secret report to Brigadier Crockett at the War Office, with another copy also sent to Colonel Teague of ISLD. It was the interrogation report of Sergeant E. Neuzbacher (Neussbacher). Nussbacher was also known as **Joel Palgi**. His code names were MICKY and HULBERT. [1]

Simonds wrote that he was enclosing two copies of Nussbacher's (Palgi's) full interrogation report and reiterated that the agent had been sent to Yugoslavia so as to penetrate Hungary and organize escape activities there. He had returned to Cairo on June 23, 1945. [2]

Simonds stated that it was an interesting narrative and contained the full account of all the events which had affected the following MI9 and ISLD agents: [3]

MI9
Miss Hannah Senesh ("MINNIE")
Sgt. Neuzbacher ("MICKY" and 'HULBERT")

ISLD
Sgt. Goldstein ("JONES")
Sgt. Rosenfeld ("DICKENS")
Sgt. Granville ("MAGISTRATE")
ALBERT

ISLD agent Albert's name had been underlined, as it appears above. [4]

Due to the fact that Nussbacher (Palgi) still had relatives in Russian-occupied Hungary, it was requested that the interrogation report be considered especially TOP SECRET. It was also clear that it contained information of a highly sensitive nature. [5]

The report included the following details pertaining to Gabor Haraszty, a.k.a. ALBERT: [6]

1. ALBERT had arrived in Yugoslavia in May 1944, with important information.

2. Major Eden had gone to Casma to meet ALBERT.

3. The Gestapo and Hungarian Counter-Intelligence were aware of the British agent ALBERT and had mistaken Nussbacher (Palgi) for him while he was imprisoned.

4. The Gestapo claimed to have evidence that ALBERT had recently gone from Budapest to the partisan area of Yugoslavia and then returned.

5. ALBERT Operations had been linked to CHICKEN (Jewish rescue) Operations.

6. To avoid further torture, Palgi had to sign everything they put in front of him, accusing him of being the British agent ALBERT.

7. Palgi's intention had been to tell them at his trial that he was not ALBERT and had been forced to sign the confession. But, as the trial was indefinitely postponed, he did not have a chance to do so.

8. After his escape, Palgi had been helped by the RAF Airman "Tim," who was in direct contact with ISLD in Budapest. "Tim" was staying at the villa of Dr. Antal, as were other POWs. * He was also in touch with the Jewish Underground, and was getting ready to leave the capital.

* RAF airman Reginald Barratt, known as TIM, was staying at the villa of Dr. Antal at the same time Palgi met TIM the RAF airman. It was the villa on Narcisz Street, which Palgi later referred to as "Narcissus Street" in his (English) published memoirs.

PALGI'S RELEASE

Prior to his release from the British military into civilian life in British-occupied Palestine, Joel Palgi - a.k.a. Nussbacher - was required to sign a certificate of discharge, which included the following sentence. [7]

"What information, knowledge, facts, details or any other matters I have gleaned or obtained during the fulfillment of my duties ... are not to be disclosed to any unauthorized persons on my discharge from the service, in accordance with the Official Service Act 1911 and 1920, which I have read and studied in detail." [8]

The correspondence of MI9 on the previous day implied that the British were quite anxious to speed up his discharge, as he had "returned from a long period of continuous and highly secret operations," and it was thus preferred he not have "contact with any others in the camp." [9]

It is also worthy of mention that, despite Palgi's request, his certificate of release did not disclose whether he had worked at an office for the duration of his service or if he had been an active field agent in the theater of the Second World War. [10]

Notes:

1. WO 208/3405 *(MI9 personnel file of Nussbacher (Palgi), with reports)*
2. Ibid
3. Ibid
4. Ibid
5. Ibid
6. Ibid
7. Ibid
8. Ibid
9. Ibid
10. Ibid

CHAPTER 18
THE ENGLISH PATIENT

Count Laszlo Almasy - the romantic Hungarian explorer featured in *The English Patient* [1] - was also reported to have had contact with British Intelligence.

Almasy too played a role in the Hungarian Boy Scouts movement. In 1933, the 4th World Scout Jamboree was held in Hungary. It was one year after Karoly and his friends had met "Jack," the future British agent, at a Boy Scouts jamboree in Poland. One of the Hungarian scout leaders in 1933 was Laszlo Almasy, who escorted Baden-Powell on his official visit.

In 1939, the British-educated Almasy was said to have offered his services to the British armed forces in Egypt - as a desert adviser. [2]

Later, as a reservist and flight instructor in the Hungarian Air Force, Almasy did not go unnoticed by the Germans in Budapest. But the real English Patient was neither a Nazi nor a German agent. [3] As a reservist captain in the Hungarian Air Force, he was simply ordered to become a member of the German Afrika Korps. [4] Though he always considered himself first and foremost a Hungarian, his talents were soon put to use by the Abwehr, German military intelligence. His most famous mission was Operation Salaam, in which he transported two German spies to Egypt from Libya.[5]

According to some accounts, in 1943, while in Turkey, Almasy may have become a double agent for British intelligence. There were rumors of his having operated a clandestine radio for MI6 in the Hungarian capital. [6]

During the worst times of Nazi-occupied Budapest in 1944, he saved some Jewish Hungarians by hiding them in his apartment. He also came to the assistance of an Olympic fencing champion of Jewish origin, by procuring Swedish passports for his family and taking them to one of Wallenberg's safe houses.[7]

The Almasy mansion was located at 29 Miklos Horthy Ave *, adjacent to the Gellert Hotel. Almasy occupied a flat on the ground floor.

It was a mere ten minute walk from the Almasy mansion to the Swedish Legation, the Schandl villa, and a five minute walk to the Cave Church.

* Miklos Horthy Ave has since been renamed Bartok Bela ut.

Following the siege of Budapest, Almasy was taken to the Hungarian Communist Secret Police (AVO/AVH) Headquarters at 60 Andrassy Street, for a brutal interrogation. After eight months of suffering and a trial in which he was found not guilty of having been a Nazi, he was finally released. At the time, he weighed 90 lbs.[8]

Two months later, the British-educated Almasy was once again a person of interest for the Communists – specifically the NKVD. He was again imprisoned at 60 Andrassy Street and interrogated concerning his links to Western intelligence. The order had come from Moscow.[9]

But the West was not about to abandon him.

It is believed that at the instigation of the British, a cousin of Egypt's King Farouk delivered a bribe to the Hungarians, to secure his "escape." Details of Almasy's "escape" remain unknown. What is known, however, is that he was transported to the British zone of Vienna, the British consulate in Trieste, and was then provided with British travel documents and an air ticket from Rome to Cairo. It was an agent of the Secret Intelligence Service (MI6) who oversaw his safe arrival in Cairo, and reportedly threw the NKVD off his trail.[10]

The real English patient spent his remaining years in Egypt and became Director of the Cairo Desert Institute. Following his death from dysentery in 1951, his private papers mysteriously disappeared from his Cairo apartment. [11]

Notes:

1. Michael Ondaatje, *The English Patient* (Vintage 1993)
2. John Bierman, *The Secret Life of Laszlo Almasy: The Real English Patient* (Penguin Books 2004)
3. Török, Zsolt :'László Almásy: *The Hungarian explorer of the unknown Sahara, in* : Földrajzi Közlemények, (1997), Vol. CXXI., No. 1-2, pp. 77 – 86
4. Ibid
5. Ibid
6. John Bierman, *The Secret Life of Laszlo Almasy: The Real English Patient* (Penguin Books 2004)
7. Ibid
8. Ibid
9. Ibid
10. Ibid
11. Ibid

PART II
COLD WAR

CHAPTER 19
LUBYANKA

LUBYANKA PRISON
Moscow, 1945

The NKVD/SMERSH had put Karoly Schandl and Gerit Van der Waals in the notorious Lubyanka and Lefortovo prisons.

If a group of Canadian and American airmen in Bucharest hasn't noticed them being taken away by the Russians, under heavily armed guard (along with members of the Abwehr), no one would have known they were there. [1]

Karoly's cellmate for the next year was to be Gerit Van der Waals, with whom he had been arrested. At the beginning, they were not permitted to sleep. The sounds that were played into the room, as well as the extreme heat and cold they soon experienced, were intolerable. [2]

At the beginning, Karoly and Van der Waals also underwent tough interrogation procedures, during which they were occasionally separated.

The tactics included mind games. [3]

The following 7 pages are from the private writings of Karoly Schandl, in which he describes scenes from his own prison interrogations.

INTERROGATIONS

He had not been asleep very long when a sergeant entered the cell, with another guard at the door.

"Get dressed."

He grasped for his clothes.

"Hurry up."

He did.

"Hands back."

They led him through a maze of corridors to a simply furnished room.

There was a table, behind it two officers.

"Your name?"

He answered and the younger officer took over. "You are a spy."

"No, I am not."

"Prove that you are not a spy."

"How?"

"By telling us everything."

"You must have made a mistake. You took me for somebody else."

The older officer shouted a curse.

"If you do not cooperate, you will be shot. If you cooperate, you may get away with a lighter sentence."

"What information did you provide and whom did you meet in the organization?"

"I don't know about information."

They looked at him with stern and menacing faces. The younger officer then called for the two sergeants.

He was relieved when they arrived and he was allowed to leave.

"Ruky nazad. Put your hands back and hurry up."

They led him back to his cell.

THE SPY

He did not see anything of Moscow except for the sky

from the enclosure where they were taken for their daily walk - never at the same time.

The sky was always different.

Early in the morning, it was dark gray, and millions of crows were flying around. Dark masses, circling and crying above.

One day, the door of his cell opened and a tall man was escorted in.

The man in city clothing was clean, cultured looking.

He put down his mattress, his sheets, towel, and cover, arranging it all neatly, sat down, and took out some cigarettes.

"Do you smoke?" were his first words.

He accepted the cigarette to be polite but did not smoke it.

The newcomer lit his. "I am Alexei. Why were you arrested?"

"They say that I am a spy."

"Is it true?"

"No. They must think I am someone else."

"Naturally," Alexei replied. "Everybody says so."

"No, really."

"Alright, you don't have to tell me about it unless you want to."

The newcomer was talkative.

"My friend, I am an American spy. I don't deny it. Instead, I told them everything. I have to save my skin."

He nodded.

Alexei went on. "I told them about the scoundrel Petrov. He was the agent who recruited me. He gave me money, plenty of money, a truck and a radio transmitter. With my brother, who is also here, we had to travel along the river and report on the traffic on the river. Count the ships, the barges, and guess what they carry. With our truck, we followed the road on the river, from town to town. It was a good life. Plenty of money, plenty of girls. God only knows the real names of the American agents - but they always operate under a very common name."

Alexei paused "And how did you live? Who was your contact?"

He replied that he did not have any such spy contacts.

Alexei continued. "And when they are tired of you, or they think that you operated long enough, they send an anonymous letter to the NKVD. They betray their agents, change their name, move to another city, and start from scratch. It is a spiteful thing.

But I will repay everything. I will see that they get the swine Petrov, or whatever his real name is. I want to see him hanged.

I will get away with a light sentence, because I cooperated fully with my investigators. Besides, I did not know that I was spying. I thought we were providing information, confidential information."

Time went fast now that he was not alone.

Around midnight, an officer with a sergeant appeared. By now, he knew his interrogation would continue.

He was right. They led him to the elevator, down a few floors, through corridors, through an iron door, controlled by a junior officer, to the same room where he had been earlier.

The same two officers as before. They looked at him sternly.

"Sit down. Did you think it over?"

His face was blank.

"Tell us everything you know."

"I don't know anything."

"Don't lie, you scoundrel! You will rot in your own dung in the jails, you rotten louse! And you will be transported to another prison, where we have more control. You will pay for your lies!" The older, senior Officer hit the table several times and cursed menacingly.

Finally the subaltern officer and the sergeant who had brought him there arrived.

He was allowed to leave, and was escorted back to his cell.

His cellmate was gone, with all his belongings.

The next day was difficult. He was sleepy and tired. He was not allowed to close his eyes, he had to sit on the bed. In the neighboring cells, the inmates made the same steps.

After an hour of sleep, during the early part of the night, they came again. This time he was led to the same area where he had spent the first days.

They searched him and he was directed to the Black Crow, the truck for prisoners.

He was in a daze, but realized that the truck was leaving Lubyanka. The big gate opened and slammed. They turned left and right. He heard the noise of traffic, horns, stops and starts.

After a trip of about half an hour, the slamming of another gate.

He had arrived in the Lefortovo prison.

He went through the ritual of being searched, having a shower, waiting naked while his clothes were in the disinfecting oven.

Then he was led inside. A big building with cement floors, three stories high. The inside of the building, with four wings, all visible from the center area separated by mesh, to prevent people from jumping to their death from the open corridors. Staircases, circular iron stairs.

In the center area was a sergeant with two assistants, sitting at a table. The sergeant was signaling with a green flag to the incoming group, led by a sergeant, followed by the young man with his load of a thin mattress, carrying also his pillowcase and blanket, trying to keep his pants from falling down. He was followed by another guard.

They entered through an iron door on the ground floor. The green flag was shown to another wing. The sergeant in the middle directed the traffic to prevent the prisoners from seeing each other.

Finally, they arrived at cell no. 111, on the second floor, in the corner of one of the wings. The cell was somewhat bigger than the cell he'd had in the Lubyanka. It was also older. The walls were uneven, the cement floor old and worn.

The door was painted dark green, but there was also a structure in the corner by the door – the toilet. And a water tap with a small basin, the water flowing from it directly to the toilet.

An iron bed, with wooden planks.

He put down his thin mattress, covered it with a sheet, and lay down.

There was a guard watching him through the spy hole. The guard opened the square flap in the door and ordered him to turn around.

His head was in the wrong direction. He had to face the door, to be seen. He followed the order. Just above the door was the bare light bulb, shining in his eyes during the whole night.

Opposite the door, high up so that he could not reach it, was a dirty window, the glass fortified by mesh, and sheltered from outside by sheet metal. If he made an effort and the upper part of the window was opened to the inside, he could see a minute portion of the sky.

Everything was one scale below the standards of the Lubyanka.

What in the Lubyanka was done by junior officers, here was done by sergeants.

There were the sounds of motors roaring outside his window. They had to be next to a place were engines were tested and "run in."

He had his open air walk not on the top of the building, but in a closed yard. The yard was subdivided into eight sections, each about twelve by fifteen feet, separated from each other by wooden walls, about fifteen feet high.

The guard supervising him was walking the length of the structure on a wooden plank.

In the mornings, the guard was clapping the little flaps on the door, the flaps that closed the square opening that was cut in the door for food and communications. Clap, clap, clap, throughout the whole building. Everybody had to get up.

Outside the window, high, close to the roof, there were

loudspeakers. Loudspeakers also on the inside of the big hall, filling out the big shell. The cell, at least the faded window of it, faced the courtyard where the structure for the daily walk was standing.

And the loudspeakers were telling the English spies they were going to die.

The neighbor – or neighbors – in cell no. 110 were walking in their cell. Above the cell there was also movement.

HEARINGS

The prison came to life as the time to take the prisoners for interrogation approached.

They escorted him to the ground floor, to an iron door, and passed through it. He found himself in a somber looking room with two "kommissars," his previous investigators, seated behind a table.

"Sit down. Did you think it over? Are you willing to talk?"

"I told you everything I know."

"All lies, all lies. We want to know the truth."

"It is the truth."

"Look here you idiot. We have a report from a reliable source that you are an English agent. He knows about your activities and the trips. He is a trustworthy man."

"He must be a liar."

"Shut up you son of a bitch, you miserable liar!" interrupted the older investigator.

"You will see what will happen to you if you try to fool with us," followed the younger one.

He sat in silence.

Then the younger officer took three photos from the folder. "Do you know these people?"

He looked at the photographs.

Three faces. One of them was Alexei, the man who was with him in Lubyanka, the others were just ordinary faces that he had never seen before.

"I recognize him. He is Alexei."
"Were you working with him?"
"No, he was in my cell in the Lubyanka."
"What did he tell you?"
"That he worked for an American agent. I think he called him Petrov."
"He was lying to you, he worked for the same American agent as you!"
"Don't lie, you miserable bastard," interrupted the older officer.

The younger one took over.
"Do you know what happened to this Alexei?"
"No, he was not in the cell when I returned."
"He was shot yesterday. He tried to lie to us, like you do."

He was visibly shaken.
They seemed to be satisfied.
"Why were you spying? Why were you gathering information?"
"I did not gather information."
The younger Officer made notes, and finally said "We don't believe you, but now our Control Department will take over your case."
"And you will crawl on the floor of your cell asking to be shot, you son of a bitch," added the older Officer. [4]

WORRIES

Despite his own predicament, Karoly was worried about his family back in Budapest - and rightfully so. In late December, Sister Sara Salkahazi of the Bokreta home, a nun with whom Terezia Schandl had been collaborating, was executed by the Arrow Cross. The fascists had discovered a Jewish boy hiding in the guard's booth of the Bokreta home. Terezia, as a member of the board, had hidden Jewish refugees in the home after providing them with false identities and pretending they were domestic helpers. The Arrow Cross vowed to round up all members of the board the following day, but were prevented from doing so when the Russians reached the city and engaged the Arrow Cross in heavy fighting (see Terezia's memoirs in *Sword of the Turul*). *Sister Sara Salkahazi was beatified in 2005 (AP).*

SECRET PRISONERS

In the early days of his Russian captivity, Karoly Schandl communicated with Raoul Wallenberg using Morse code. One day, however, the communication came to an end and the guard informed him that the prisoner next door had "died." [5]

Karoly assumed the information was accurate. After all, he bore witness early on to the cruelty of his captors. After a year in his cell in the Lefortovo Prison, the tortured Gerit Van der Waals was moved to another cell on the same floor. Karoly never saw him again and heard that not long after, the young Dutch lieutenant had committed suicide by hanging himself. [6]

Schandl had been arrested during the Second World War, had been transported to Moscow under heavily armed guard, and was kept under the most brutal and secretive conditions.

"All of those poor people who died in that place," he

later lamented.

In 1947, the Russians informed the Swedish government that they knew nothing about Raoul Wallenberg, who had gone missing in Budapest after coming into contact with the occupying Red Army.[7] This was typical of their approach. They had denied holding Gerit Van der Waals captive, just as they had denied knowing the whereabouts of Karoly Schandl, whose parents had asked after him repeatedly when he failed to return to Budapest.

They weren't the only ones who had been secretly arrested by the NKVD.

According to Soviet logic, anyone who had come into contact with any organization suspected of being a spy organization must therefore be a spy. As a result, members of the armed anti-Nazi resistance were arrested in Hungary in the early days of the Russian occupation in 1945, as were Zionist activists. Those who were treated the most harshly included individuals who had been involved in intelligence, counter-intelligence, and dealings with foreign firms.[8]

This information was certainly known by the Allies.

In fact, it was said by some Hungarians that in 1948, the British Foreign Secretary had a "serious exchange" concerning the fate of a group of British officers who had been killed by the Soviets in the vicinity of Hungary just after the war, though the details of the communications regarding the matter were never made public ...

Notes:

1. C. Schandl, *Sword of the Turul* (Lulu Press 2005)
2. Ibid
3. Ibid
4. *7 page Excerpt from the Private Writings of Karoly Schandl*
5. C. Schandl, *Sword of the Turul* (Lulu Press 2005)
6. Ibid
7. *The Other Side of the Wall* (Time Magazine, Monday, March 2, 1953)
8. Krisztian Ungvary, *The Siege of Budapest: 100 Days in World War II* (I.B. Taurus 2002, Yale University Press 2005)

CHAPTER 20
ISOLATION

Schandl's parents had tried unsuccessfully for years to learn what had become of their missing son. Though unaware of the details, they had known that he had been helping the British during the War. He had informed his parents just before departing in December 1944, that he was taking a "British agent" across the front lines, as per his orders.

In 1950, Karoly's parents were arrested by the AVO/AVH, Hungarian Communist Secret police and placed in separate jails for two years. It had been a set up. [1]

Interestingly, 1950 was also the year that Karoly had another hearing in the Lubyanka prison, though to the outside world, he no longer existed. [2]

"In February 1950, after my 'official' arrest in January 1950, ordered by General Abakumov - who was shot four years later - I was transferred for a 'hearing' to the Lubyanka Prison from the Lefortovo. It was a change. In the Lubyanka I had to wait 48 hours before my hearing by Lt. Simonov, who worked as interpreter with Major Shidorov (Sidorov?)." [3]

Karoly's Soviet captors tried to trick him into admitting he knew Laszlo Pap (Papp), via a photograph with Pap's name written on the back [4]

Laszlo Pap had been in the same group as Karoly in World War II Hungary, helping their "common friend" Gabor Haraszty (British agent ALBERT). Pap was a young Hungarian in the same prison. He too had been working with Haraszty's group. [5]

The group had been not only helping Allied POWs,

but also gathering military intelligence for the Allies.

Considering that Gabor Haraszty had reportedly been killed by the NKVD approximately 5 years earlier, the Soviets' fixation on the activities of his group did seem rather unusual.

Karoly's hearing did not last long.

He had already been shown part of the evidence which had been given against him. There were 5 reports of 5 testimonies, each one signed. Four were from contacts who pretended not to have known him. But the fifth one was interesting. It was detailed and criticized him for gathering intelligence, taking trips, not supporting the communist cause, and having had suspicious contact with an American spy - among other things.

He was furious.

He could almost hear the man taunting him - that none of his contacts would be able to help him now ...

During the night-time hearing, Karoly was not given a chance to speak.

The final outcome was something of a shock.

He was sentenced to 25 years in prison for having had contact with an anti-Soviet organization for the purpose of spying - the British Intelligence Service.

It all seemed to have been prearranged.

Shortly after the verdict, Karoly was transported to Vladimir prison. Vladimir prison was considered the most highly secretive prison of the Soviet Union, for high profile prisoners. Karoly was baffled. He had simply been helping the Allies in Hungary during the Second World War. [6]

Just as he had arrived in Moscow - under heavily armed guard - he was transported to Vladimir by stony faced armed guards, accompanied by guard dogs. Other prisoners were transported at the same time. As they approached the train, for a moment he considered breaking free and throwing himself onto the tracks. But he changed his mind and reminded himself that despite the dire circumstances, at least he was still alive. Perhaps he had come this far for a reason. [7]

Once they had reached Vladimir prison, he was placed in isolation and assigned a number in lieu of his name, so that no one would be aware of his real identity.

There were two other Hungarians secretly held in the same section – Laszlo Pap and Tibor Clement/Klement. [8]

The special section was a terrible place to be, as there were microphones and ultrasonic sounds used to exert pressure on the prisoners as the mind games and intimidation tactics continued. [9]

Life and Death

To the left of the cell, when he was facing the high windows which were covered from the outside with sheet metal to prevent them from climbing up and looking out, there was a sick, old man in solitary. The "doctorcha" visited him daily, and he received medication three times a day.

He got weaker each day until one evening there was a big commotion, because the sick man said he was unable to make it to the washroom. The sergeant argued with him but he refused to go. Finally they dragged him along the floor, with a guard carrying his "paracha."

He did not live long after this.

One day when the guards changed, the outgoing guard told the next one "He died."

The same day they took away the body.

He later learned that they had to pierce the heart of a dead body, in the presence of the doctors and the commander of the prison, before it was shipped to a medical school, if there was one within reach. If there was none, they incinerated it. And the person's file was closed.

He soon learned that there were living people behind the speakers who operated the input. On one occasion, the night guard phoned somebody early in the night. "You don't have to listen. I am looking." On another occasion, there was the sound of music, probably from a radio, enjoyed, it seemed, by the operators. Then suddenly somebody said "He's coming," and the music was switched off and they began the usual, mostly meaningless talk of the recordings. [10]

Karoly Schandl

Time passed slowly but then one day, in 1952, there was an unexpected commotion.

ZIONISTS IN VLADIMIR

The prisoners learned about a process against some Jewish doctors in Moscow who had been accused of being in contact with an international Zionist organization. A few weeks later, two newcomers arrived in their section.
One of them was evidently upset about the whole thing. On the evening of his arrival, he was shouting. "I am a doctor, I am a bocher. I attended international conferences in Brazil. I am a well known man!"
Another new arrival, somebody in the same group, shouted back at him.
Evidently they had "incriminated" each other.
The sergeant and the guards ended the shouting match and the newcomers disappeared for two days, probably into the "carcer," a dark hole. It was just 6 by 4 feet, with a cement block to sit and sleep on. Half of the usual bread portion and water. That's all. In complete darkness.
A few days later, the same doctor loudly complained that they wouldn't let him sleep in his cell.
"Let me sleep. I cannot sleep. What law permits you to torture me?"
He(Karoly) knew the feeling.
One sunny afternoon, during summer, he was listening to beautiful music. It seemed the music lovers were operating

the loudspeakers. "La donna e mobile." A nice baritone voice was singing.

The bocher doctor was singing it too, in his solitary exuberance.

That meant the sound system was common, if not for the whole prison or building, at least for their section. [11]

Karoly Schandl

POTYAMA

Not long after Stalin died, Karoly was placed in the general section and then abruptly one day told that he was being moved ...

They were shipped to the same station where they had arrived years earlier. The three of them were handled together and boarded a prison coach, together in a compartment.

The guards were less secretive with them than they had been when he was sent to Vladimir. Through the door, they could observe the landscape.

In the morning, they could see flat lands, a few trees and a big river, occasionally some barges on it. At stations, they could see people, and other trains.

They were on the line to Siberia. Their coach was left behind at a bigger station and they could see the signs. Rjasan. They were being taken to Potyama.

There was a country of prison camps around Potyama, south of Gorky and the Volga. There were more than 40 camps, all constructed in the twenties. There were 3 or 4 camps for women, and one for children. They were famous for their lack of food. One of the group had already been in no. 12 before he was sent to jail in Vladimir.

He told them about the camps.

There were about 2000-5000 inmates in a camp, housed in barn-like houses, each with 2 or 3 rooms, and in each big room about 100 to 120 people, sleeping on double or triple bunks. If there, it was best to try and get on the top bunk, because they were warmer in the winter. It was true that they could be dangerous. A fellow once rolled off a top bunk and broke his neck. Naturally, if you were sick and had to go to the paracha during the night, it was not advisable to be over others. They might kill you if you disturbed them during the night.

They could observe the sandy soil and birch forest south of the line, once they left the yellow, sandy meadows and crippled cornfields around Rjasan.

It was around noon that they saw the first prison camps. Observation towers with armed guards, and wooden barriers around 15 feet high. The camps had their railway siding, not only for the traffic of new inmates, but also for the delivery of coal, equipment, and food.

This would be their new home for the next years, and perhaps the last place they would ever see. [12]

Karoly Schandl

As luck would have it, the camp in Mordova was not the last place Karoly Schandl would ever see. By 1956, he found himself back in Hungary, prepared to make his final escape … [13]

Notes:

1. C. Schandl, *Sword of the Turul* (Lulu Press 2005)
2. Ibid
3. C. Schandl, *Sword of the Turul* (Lulu Press 2005)
   see excerpt from Karoly Schandl's memoirs
4. Ibid
5. Ibid
6. C. Schandl, *Sword of the Turul* (Lulu Press 2005)
7. Ibid
8. Marvin W. Makinen and Ari D. Kaplan, *Cell Occupancy Analysis of Korpus 2 of the Vladimir Prison* (Report Submitted to the Swedish-Russian Working Group on the Fate of Raoul Wallenberg December 15, 2000)
   see "Schandel, Pap, Klement"
9. C. Schandl, *Sword of the Turul* (Lulu Press 2005)
10. *Excerpt from the private writings of Karoly Schandl*
11. Ibid
12. Ibid
13. C. Schandl, *Sword of the Turul* (Lulu Press 2005)

CHAPTER 21
THE SWEDES

In 1958, when a representative of the Swedish Government requested a meeting with Karoly Schandl in Canada, he agreed.

The Swedish representative was reportedly seeking information on possible Swedish citizens held in Soviet captivity.

Schandl was living in Canada as a landed immigrant, and had not yet received Canadian citizenship, which meant that he was still technically a citizen of the Hungarian People's Republic. He was working as a student in accounts and was a short time away from obtaining his designation as a Chartered Accountant in Canada. He would soon be a university professor, and set out to do what he had dreamt of for years - he was going to become average.

He had just gotten engaged and had plans to start a family.

In 1958, Karoly Schandl still had reasons to be guarded ...

- The Hungarian Communist government had imprisoned his parents for two years in 1950 and had confiscated their homes and properties. His father, Dr. Schandl, had been disdainfully referred to by the Communist Secret Police as a "royal adviser." The family was still classified as "Osztaly Idegen" - Class Aliens (undesirables) - which meant they could at any time be imprisoned again, or worse. Furthermore, the

Hungarian Communist government had refused to let them leave the country despite their repeated requests. Terezia Schandl's letters to her son indicated that they had no freedom of movement. [1]

- Karoly was desperate to help his parents out of Hungary. [2]

- He had a number of friends and relatives still living in Soviet-occupied Hungary. The friends included Karoly Haraszty (the brother of Gabor Haraszty), who had been a classmate and good friend.

- Certain events had made it apparent that even in 1956, just after his release, Karoly had still been a person of interest for the Russians. Shortly after his release, they had come looking for him again and had he not escaped after the 1956 revolution, when the borders were possible to cross, he likely would have been caught and taken back to the Soviet Union – or worse. [3]

- In December 1956, while living in England, he had ventured to Whitehall several times, yet they had not been willing to listen to him. This dismissal by Whitehall was a defining moment in his life. It was evident that no international support of any kind could be expected from the British, who had, in Karoly's mind, instructed Gabor Haraszty and his group to report to the Russians, knowing fully well what the outcome would be. [4]

- The West had not shown any interest in pursuing Soviet war criminals, such as those responsible for the massacre of thousands of Polish officers in the forest of Katyn. Like other former prisoners of the Soviet Union, Karoly had long been aware of the Soviet responsibility for the Katyn massacre. [5]

- Sweden and Canada had the luxury of freedom, yet Hungary did not. In fact, 1958 was the same year the former pro-freedom Prime Minister Imre Nagy, hero of the 1956 revolution, was secretly tried, executed and buried by the Soviet-installed Communist machine.

Schandl cooperated with the Swedes – as much as he safely could. They had not offered any assistance or protection for his friends and relatives in Communist Hungary, though he would not have expected them to, for Sweden was not in a strong position to make demands of the Soviet empire.

What would he have told them?

He would not have been willing to compromise the remaining members of the group - or their families - by giving their names or details of their resistance activities, nor would he have said anything to endanger his own relatives in Hungary.

Nevertheless, he would surely have told the Swedish representative about the prisons, just as he'd told the Newcastle Rotary Club in February 1957, after which the Evening Sentinel newspaper in the U.K. had written the following article …

'EVENING SENTINEL - Wednesday February 27, 1957
Refugee Tells of Torture

Mental torture by ultrasonic sounds "from which there was no escape" was described by Dr. Charles W. Schandl *, a Hungarian refugee, speaking to Newcastle Rotarians yesterday on his experiences in a Russian prison.
"We were attacked with a lot of texts on ultrasonic sounds," he said. "The ultrasonic voices spoke to us

continuously. They could be felt more than they could be heard. You could have shut your eyes to a loud speaker, but not from these.

In the morning there was a sudden heat over the whole body. It made the veins of your muscles and your brain dilate. Nose-bleeding resulted, then followed a period of restlessness: sea-sickness.

After the heat period came a sudden period of stiffness, as if you were turning to stone. Sleeplessness followed."

Dr. Schandl, who is now engaged as an interpreter, was a resistance worker imprisoned by the Russians ... in 1944' [6]

* *Charles is the English translation of Karoly*

Another fact that Karoly Schandl was not secretive about was how Gerit Van der Waals, with whom he'd been arrested, had been working for the Swedish Legation in Budapest. It had been known by a number of people back then.

Did Karoly know Raoul Wallenberg?

As always, he would have claimed that he had not.

But he would certainly have remembered his own last encounter with the Soviets, just before they had released him a few years earlier, as it was not the kind of thing a man could easily forget ...

The Political Officer was sitting behind the simple wooden table, with him a young Sub-Lieutenant.

"Sit down."

He did.

"The Highest Council of the Union of Soviet Socialistic Republics has forgiven the crimes for which you were convicted, and you received amnesty as of tomorrow."

He nodded.

"I have to warn you that whatever you have seen or experienced during the process, in the jails, prison camps, during your imprisonment is a secret of the State. The breach of this secret is an indictable offense against the Soviet State. In effect, it is considered spying. So keep your silence." [7]

Karoly Schandl

Unbeknownst to the Swedes at that time, Schandl believed that Soviet intelligence had KGB plants in a number of organizations. Their arms were far reaching.

And he was right, for Vilmos Boehm - who had been active in the Allied cause during the war and then became Hungary's Ambassador to Sweden - was later discovered to have been passing information to the Soviets. [8]

Notes:

1. C. Schandl, *Sword of the Turul* (Lulu Press 2005)
2. Ibid
3. Ibid
4. Ibid
5. Ibid
6. *Evening Sentinel* (February 27, 1957)
7. *Excerpt from the private writings of Karoly Schandl*
8. S. Berger, *Stuck in Neutral: The Reasons behind Sweden's Passivity in the Raoul Wallenberg case* (August 2005)

CHAPTER 22
FROM POLAND

Canada – 1960s

When Karoly had looked up from the enclosure used for walks in the Lubyanka, in the mornings, the gray sky had been filled with masses of black crows flying overhead. And they made sounds as though they were crying – the cry of the condemned man. The crows were still there, except they no longer saw him. They surely saw others, for there were thousands of captives who at some point walked in that enclosure, with its wooden planks, barbed wire overhead, and guard with a submachine gun.

Though if you had ever been there, you would call that gun a guitar.

On a Canadian coastal town, however, everything was different. The crows did not appear to notice him here. The sky wasn't really gray, it was a bluish shade, with white clouds and mist often blocking the sun, but no one seemed to mind.

He settled down to a quiet life with his young family, and went about his routine as a university professor and family man.

There were lectures to give, exams to correct, and schedules to maintain.

Everyone, everything from the past was now gone.

His previous life had become just a story, and a rather outlandish one.

Or had it really?

For Karoly Schandl and another European man who soon crossed his path, the reality was still there.

It is not known exactly when or where he first met the Polish professor who came to the coastal town. He arrived not long after Karoly and when they walked or spoke together, one could not help but notice how comfortable they were in each other's presence.

A position had become available at the same university and the Polish professor had somehow learned of it, applied from Ireland, and had been accepted.

COLLEAGUES

He and Karoly never said from where or how exactly they knew one another.

He was rather tall, with a military stance and the manners of a European gentleman. His eyes were content, though always looking ahead, as though he expected something out of the ordinary to occur.

He refused to own a car - or even rent one - instead taking a taxi to the campus every day. And to anywhere else he would walk, regardless of how long it took.

Perhaps he was simply mindful of the fact that he too was considered an enemy of the Soviet state - and tampering with cars to cause accidents was a specialty of the KGB, not to mention that the Polish Communist Secret Police were also known for their cunning.

He was one of the heroes of the Polish resistance. As a young cadet officer of the Academic Legion of the NSZ, he had participated in the Warsaw uprising. He had fought under the AK – Polish Home Army. The professor who looked like he came from another time, another place, was known in certain circles as a hero of the Polish resistance.

He ended up living a few streets down from Karoly Schandl in a house which looked blandly North American on the outside, though on the inside it was anything but bland – or North American.

His academic works - which were not in favor of the Iron Curtain - were published worldwide and still survive today. They were published under his alias.

He considered Karoly a true friend. His Polish wife, however, was apprehensive. The suspicion she was unable to hide was evident in her posture, the pained smile, masked by good European manners. It was apparent that she would have preferred to keep a distance despite her husband's enthusiasm. The uneasiness and the wall the Polish professor's wife erected around herself, specifically for the Schandls, were not unfamiliar to Karoly. He had seen it before, when he'd finally been released into Hungary. It was the fear people had of anyone who had been imprisoned in the Soviet Union.

SUSPICION

Such was one of the problems faced by former prisoners. The first time Karoly encountered that sentiment had been in Hungary in 1956. Some people had feared being seen with him, as he may have been under surveillance. Then it later dawned on him that they also feared him. The Soviet Union was like a dark enigma to the smaller lands it had conquered. As Henry Kissinger stated, Hungary itself had become a victim of Soviet expansionism. [1] And with the totalitarian era had comes spies and plants - some within a country, others having been recruited from the ranks of past prisoners.

This was known to have occurred in wars. During the Second World War, the British had discovered Nazi spies among Germany's escaped prisoners of war, who had been permitted to "escape" only after they agreed to spy and report back to their Nazi captors. Fortunately, no such individuals were known to have come into contact with the anti-Nazi group to which Karoly and his friends belonged. Otherwise, the Nazis would have known the identity of ALBERT, yet, as indicated by Joel Palgi, the Nazis never knew ALBERT's true identity. In 1944, based on the word of a fellow prisoner, they were quick to wrongfully assume that Palgi himself was ALBERT.

It was an ironic tragedy that the real ALBERT would reportedly meet his death at the hands of the Soviets within the year.

When Raphael Rupert was released from a Soviet gulag into Hungary and fled for England, once in England, he found himself under close scrutiny by Scotland Yard and MI5 for having been a Soviet prisoner for so many years. [2]

Karoly's problems had started the moment he re-entered Hungary. Though in hiding, he still managed to contact old friends, some of whom eyed him with suspicion - probably wondering whether the prisoner had become an informer. To complicate matters, the Russians came looking for him again shortly afterwards.

He no longer belonged anywhere. Fortunately, he had anticipated their next move and had taken the necessary precautions as soon as he was released. He had stayed with a trusted friend for a few weeks, then moved to another place. While at the other place, he learned that the Russians had come to his friend's apartment several times in an attempt to find him. His freedom, it seemed, would not have lasted long, nor would his life.

Following the Hungarian revolution, his escape, and a short stay in England, he found himself in a city in Canada, and then the coastal town. There were so few Hungarians in and around the coastal town that he simply never met any, with the exception of an ambitious doctor and his wife, who soon moved west for more opportunities.

Thus, for a short time, he had been spared of the attitude towards those who had escaped from behind the Iron Curtain - until he had met the Polish professor's wife. But the professor himself paid her no mind, likely dismissing her apprehension as unnecessary.

CONNECTIONS

It is worthy of mention that the British-led resistance group with which Karoly had worked had contact with the AK (Polish Home Army). Some of Karoly's friends - like the Zerkowitz brothers - had even opened their homes to high ranking members of the AK when they were in Budapest for secret meetings. Haraszty's group was actively helping Poles, Jews, and Allied prisoners of war. And during Karoly's Soviet imprisonment, one of his cellmates for a brief time had been "Leopold," of the Polish General Staff.

As reported in *The Secret History of England's Special Operations Executive*, early on in the war, the "sentimental link" between Hungary and Poland was used by the British to encourage "work" in Poland via Hungary. British agent Clement (Klement) was dropped into Poland in 1943. Also, it should not be forgotten that a number of British-led couriers made numerous trips from Hungary to Poland to provide the Polish Underground in Warsaw with supplies, as well as radio parts which were provided by Philips.

Gerit Van der Waals, the Dutch Officer, with whom Karoly had been arrested, had been in direct contact with

Smit, the Director of Philips Radio in the Balkans. Among his other roles, Van der Waals was a "cut-out" courier who was reported to have worked for Smit.

The links to Poland and the Polish resistance were numerous. It is more than likely that the underground networks of Schandl and the Polish professor would have worked together, on some level.

The Polish professor was awarded a Virtuti Militari Cross, Poland's highest military decoration, equivalent to the British Victoria Cross. It was awarded to him by General Tadeusz Komorowski, a.k.a General Bor of the AK, commander of the Polish Underground - for "courage under fire."

Notes:

1. Henry Kissinger, *Diplomacy* (Simon and Schuster 1994)
2. Raphael Rupert, *Red Wire and the Lubianka* (Ballinakella 1991)

CHAPTER 23
THE ADDRESS BOOK

After the Russians had entered Budapest in 1945, they set about tracking down and arresting individuals believed to have had contact with intelligence, counter-intelligence, Zionists, as well as those who had done business with international companies. [1]

It did not stop simply with the individual whom they arrested. Names found in such a person's notebook would lead to the imprisonment of all persons listed in the notebook, as they had been in contact with the accused "spy." [2]

Karoly Schandl did not have a notebook of names after he'd left Hungary. He did, however, own an address book for purely personal reasons, as he was in touch with old friends, relatives, and former cellmates. [3]

FRIENDS

Among the old friends with whom he corresponded was Karoly Haraszty, Gabor's elder brother. He had been Karoly Schandl's classmate as a boy. As Karoly Haraszty remained in Hungary, the letters contained only topics which would not cause problems for him with the Communist authorities. One could write about harmless trivialities and such. Karoly Haraszty had also taken part in some of the wartime resistance activities of the group, though he had not joined the British army, as Gabor had.

Schandl spoke of Karoly Haraszty as a man of courage and intelligence.

Another old friend was Peter Zerkowitz, who ended up in New York. Peter's accomplishments within the Hungarian resistance are known by historical experts. His courage was matched by his loyalty and trustworthiness.

There was also Raphael Rupert, who had done a great deal of work with Reginald Barratt and was taken to a Soviet gulag for his efforts. His Ireland address was included.

Another name was Ferenc Vali, to whom Karoly fondly referred as Vali Pepi. He was a well known international lawyer who had been part of a Hungarian Government mission sent to make contact with the Allied powers in Istanbul during the War. He had ended up as a professor living in Amherst, Massachusetts.

Of course, Karoly Schandl's London contact, "M," was in the address book - several times, as he'd had numerous addresses.

There was also the name and address of a London-based Hungarian acquaintance who had become something of a celebrity in the U.K.

These were only a few of the many friends and acquaintances included.

RELATIONS

In addition to relatives in the United States and England, Karoly had remained in contact with certain relations in Hungary, most notably Joseph (Jozsef) Schandl, his uncle. Joseph was the younger brother of Karoly Schandl Sr. He had remained in Hungary, where he became a well known professor and genetic engineer in veterinary science and animal husbandry. His contribution to Hungarian agricultural science was so great that he was awarded the Kossuth prize, the Hungarian equivalent of the Nobel prize. Joseph lived until 1973. His bronze bust can still be found in the Budapest Museum of Agriculture. Interestingly, the bust was procured by the museum in 1954, at a time when his nephew, Karoly

Schandl, was secretly imprisoned in the Soviet Union. The Communists tended to turn a blind eye to one's family background and relations if one contributed to the fields of science and medicine.

CELLMATES

There were also former cellmates from the Soviet prisons with whom Karoly Schandl stayed in touch, including a former Polish Officer who had escaped Katyn. He had been imprisoned for even longer than Karoly. Upon his release, he abbreviated his name and settled in New York. [4]

CONTACTS

In the early 1970s, Karoly Schandl's address book disappeared under mysterious circumstances. He had placed it on the counter at the local post office when mailing Christmas cards. Within seconds, it was gone. Thus, he had to wait until the following Christmas season to re-enter the addresses of the people who wrote him letters and Christmas cards. That was how he collected the names and addresses for his replacement address book.

All of the names mentioned in this chapter appear in Karoly Schandl's newer address book. They had all sent him correspondence with their return address.

One name which never appeared in the address book was the real name or any known alias of "Jack" (a.k.a. Jacques Dubreuil), the Polish friend from the Boy Scouts jamboree who had recruited Karoly and his friends to help the British Intelligence Service during the War.

Karoly did not seem to have had any kind of contact with him following his release from Soviet captivity. However, throughout his life, he always made a point of saying that in Budapest, Gabor Haraszty had reported to "Jacques Dubreuil."

Notes:

1. Krisztian Ungvary, *The Siege of Budapest: 100 Days in World War II* (I.B. Taurus 2002, Yale University Press 2005)
2. Ibid
3. Ibid
4. Ibid

CHAPTER 24
CANADA/U.S. BORDER

Early 1970s

Karoly Schandl was going to drive his family on another one of their usual summer vacations. They had packed their suitcases, toys, and the large green picnic basket had been filled with sandwiches and soft drinks.

His wife and three kids accompanied him to the family Buick parked in the wide driveway. It was early in the morning so the crows on the street were visible, perched on the tall trees where no one could reach them. They watched with beady eyes as the family got into the car and slowly drove away.

The drive from the coastal town to the American border took several hours. As the terrain was not particularly exciting, they kept occupied by counting the cows and horses they spotted in the pastures along the highway. Of course, there were more cows than horses, and all the cows seemed to look the same.

The kids also sang as the car drove on.

This land is your land
This land is my land
From Bonavista
To Vancouver Island
From the Arctic Circle
To the Great Lake waters
This land was made for you and me.

They were on their way to visit relatives in the eastern U.S.

Everyone was excited when they finally reached the border and the tidy officers sitting behind clean booths.

Generally, they asked where one was from, where one was headed, the purpose and duration of the visit.

They pulled up to the booth and Karoly handed the young officer the passports of both himself and his wife.

"Good afternoon, sir."

He looked at the passports and asked where Karoly and his wife were from.

They replied that they had originally come from Hungary and were now Canadian citizens.

The officer then asked if either of them had ever been to the Soviet Union.

Karoly nodded. "Yes. I was in prison in Russia for almost 12 years."

The officer asked him what prisons.

"Lubyanka, Lefortovo, and Vladimir."

The officer paused and then picked up his phone to call someone. When he hung up, he asked Karoly to pull the car over to the side.

He did.

There was soon another officer standing beside the car. He was efficient in both appearance and manner as he asked everyone to get out of the car.

Meanwhile, other cars were passing by and getting through the border. Only the Schandls' car had been stopped. Everyone got out of the car and stood off to the side.

The officer asked Karoly to open the trunk.

He was not an unpleasant young man, but there was a serious air about him that made the kids stop smiling.

First he looked at the camera very carefully. He was also very interested in the boxes of film. Then he proceeded to open the suitcases and bags that had been neatly packed for the family holiday.

He was politely methodical and handled everything with care, but that didn't change the fact that only their belongings were searched. Karoly kept smiling, as if to convince his pouting kids that this was nothing out of the ordinary.

There was nothing else to do but wait for it to be over. Soon a second uniformed man came to assist. The two looked through the clothes and Barbie cases and rummaged through the picnic basket.

Meanwhile, other cars passed by and the passengers inside them stared at the spectacle.

One of the men pulled a stuffed animal from one of the bags and held it up. He then put it back and muttered something to his partner. As efficiently as they had opened the bags, they closed them and told Karoly he could drive through.

They all got back in the car and drove across the border. Everyone was silent.

The crows, it seemed, were never far behind.

CHAPTER 25
KINGSMEN OF A CENTURY

In 1980, King's College of Cambridge University published a book by Mr. Patrick Wilkinson, called *Kingsmen of a Century*. Mr. Wilkinson had himself spent 54 years at King's College, including positions as a Lay Dean, Vice-Provost, and member of the classical staff. *Kingsmen of a Century* was a well researched account of 1300 Kingsmen of note between the years 1873 and 1973, hence the book's title.[1]

It included the following entry, on page 295.

"C.W. Schandl (student of 1936), a lawyer by training, assisted the Allies clandestinely against the Nazis in his native Hungary during The War. In 1945 he was arrested by the Russians and imprisoned for ... years at Moscow for being in touch with the Intelligence Service of their own ally the British. On his release, he came over and served as an interpreter for the British Coal Board, then emigrated to Canada and became a chartered accountant. Now he is Professor..." [2]

So, in 1980, the first publication appeared, indicating that Karoly Schandl (C.W. Schandl) had been imprisoned by the Russians for having worked with the British Intelligence Service. Wilkinson's book is still considered a reference for social historians as well as past and present members of the college.[3]

The world was slowly changing – at least for most.

The early 1980s marked Karoly's relocation with his family to a big city.

In the United States, the early 1980s marked not only Ronald Reagan's rise to power, but also the hard work and determination of a Hungarian researcher who'd ended up at a prestigious American University.

Acquainted with a number of former prominent Hungarians, she also knew some of Karoly Schandl's contacts - and set about interviewing them for the Oral History archives. It was a commendable undertaking and its participants were guaranteed that none of their interview transcripts would be released without careful consideration of the applicant. Nevertheless, it should be mentioned that anyone involved in activities of a clandestine nature would never have been completely forthcoming, particularly if any friends or relations remained behind the Iron Curtain. Thus, certain names, aliases, and details would have been carefully omitted amid the exciting true stories.

As everything Hungarian in nature, the news of the worthwhile and successful project would have traveled fast.

Was it then a coincidence that "M" was suddenly compelled one day to catch a last minute flight from the U.K. to Canada, to speak with Karoly in person in lieu of using the telephone or writing the usual letter? He had never before felt the desire to visit him in Canada.

What precisely was his role? It is known that he was from Karoly's past and had been in London at the end of the war, re-appearing as one of his old contacts only in the 1960s. Karoly had simply not mentioned him until that time.

In addition ...

In the Piarist Boy Scouts in Hungary, "M" had been a member of the same small Scouts squad as Karoly Schandl, Gabor Haraszty, and Karoly Haraszty.

In the early 1950s, his nationality was listed as citizen of the British Commonwealth, outside the U.K.

By 1950, he had already become a well known sugar planter of the British West Indies, where he was a resident.

He made a number of voyages between The U.K., New York, and the West Indies during the 1950s.

He took some voyages on the steamship of the United Fruit Company.
The United Fruit Company was reportedly connected to American Intelligence.

By the 1970s, he was a resident of London, and spent a great deal of time in Africa.

He and Karoly Schandl had a number of mutual Hungarian acquaintances.

He was extremely familiar with what had been happening at the Schandl villa during the War, as only an insider would have been.

Schandl had first introduced his family to "M" in the 1970s, the first time they had visited the U.K. He had cultivated the image of an Englishman almost to perfection and was always polite.
In truth, he was something of an enigma.

One summer day in the early 1980s, Karoly announced that the guest room should be prepared, as his old acquaintance was arriving for a brief visit. The reasons for his impromptu visit were never given.

He arrived in the evening, dressed as a proper Englishman. As always, he spoke in English, with no trace of an accent.

As soon as he arrived, he asked Karoly to "go for a walk." Karoly agreed. When they returned from the walk, approximately a half hour later, "M" was visibly relieved.

Karoly later showed his wife what he had presented him with.

There were two distinct small crosses.

From the look on his face, it was evident they held some meaning which only certain parties would have understood.

"M" had apparently passed on some sort of secret message with those two crosses, but what was it? And from whom exactly?

Karoly never said why he had been given those crosses. A few days later, "M" took his leave.

When he was gone, Karoly became seriously silent for a while and smoked several pipes in the living room.

Eventually he came out of the room with a look of contentment on his face, as if in his mind, he had successfully found a way to handle a certain matter.

"I am going to write a story," he announced.

And so he got to work on his cryptic writings, which described the experiences of a young accountant who had been unjustly arrested and imprisoned by the Russians.

He would later state that he had included some of his own experiences within the story, which would later be found to have included MI9 codes.

Schandl's story - together with other personal writings - revealed that he had been gathering information for a resistance group and the Russians had arrested him for his "suspicious" activities. The Russians believed that, like others, he had been working for a "big American spy." They were also aware of the contact he'd had with an important Colonel.

And, as previously mentioned, they knew that his group had been connected to "Chicken" operations - the planned operations of courageous Zionists from Palestine.

Notes:

1. L.P. Wilkinson, *Kingsmen of a Century 1873-1972*
 (King's College, Cambridge University Press 1980, 1981)
2. Ibid
3. Ibid

CHAPTER 26
IN HIS WORDS

Canada 1990

It was a cold and windy February day. As the people streamed into the elegant funeral home, one had the feeling of having been transported back in time. Solemn men with dark European suits outnumbered the North Americans in the crowd, a few having been accompanied by their well groomed wives. They carried themselves with such dignity, one would have almost expected Count Bethlen to be among them. But he was not, nor was Karoly Schandl Senior or Junior, nor Terezia Schandl.

Karoly Schandl Junior was 77 years old when he passed away on a cold winter day in 1990, though if one subtracted the 12 years of captive hellishness he had survived, it really came to 65 years of life.

The tall, aged man who gave Karoly's eulogy was an old school friend from the Piarist high school in Budapest, who had also ended up in North America. He said Karoly had been the "wise one" among his classmates, the "keeper of the peace." He mentioned his years in Soviet captivity and then brought up the yacht club where the Boy Scouts group used to sail in the old days.

The Tihany yacht club.

"You will be my sailing partner for life," he concluded, choking back his tears.

Karoly lay in the casket, his face serene, as the priest then continued with the service. He was wearing his dark pin striped suit the formal, impeccable way only Europeans can.

The same kind of suit he'd been wearing some years

earlier, for dinner at a local Hungarian restaurant.

Flashback

"This restaurant now has a Chinese owner," he had pointed out as they sat down, a twinkle in his eye. "We shall see how Hungarian the food is now."

Everyone opened a menu.

After a brief time, Karoly put his menu on the table, having opted for cabbage rolls. The party waited for the waitress to return, but she was nowhere in sight.

The room was dim, the décor bordering somewhere between elegance and old world country charm.

One of his descendants then brought up a film which had been shown on television.

"It was about Raoul Wallenberg, the Swedish hero who saved thousands of lives during the war. It is interesting that he was in Hungary."

"Yes."

"Did you watch the movie on TV?"

"Of course."

"Did you hear anything about Raoul Wallenberg in Hungary?"

"The Swedish Legation was just across from my home in Budapest."

They were amazed. This was the first time they had ever heard of it, though he had already discussed his earlier days with his wife a long time ago.

"Dad, is it true he went missing in Hungary?"

"He did not go missing." Pause. "The Russians took him away."

"The movie said he was last seen in Budapest," they said with the optimism of inexperienced North Americans. "Maybe he'll be found one day."

"The Russians claimed they killed him. That's what the guard told me in the prison. They said they shot him. Everyone in the Lubyanka knew it back then." He sounded exasperated and then described what had happened. At the beginning of his own captivity, Karoly had communicated with the Swedish diplomat using Morse code on the wall, and it sounded as though he had been in the cell next to him. It went on for quite some time, though Karoly did not reveal what they discussed. Then one day the tapping stopped. He had asked the guard what happened to him.

"He died," was the response.

He later heard that it was being reported by the guards in the prison that Raoul Wallenberg had been executed - shot, to be exact.

You could not have convinced Karoly Schandl that it wasn't true, but how reliable were the guards and how did one know whether they were simply following orders by "reporting" to others whatever it was the Soviet authorities wished to be known?

"Did you know Raoul Wallenberg in Budapest?"

He shook his head. "No. But Van der Waals worked for him. He made IDs for people so that they could escape Nazi persecution. Raoul Wallenberg paid him every month."

That was what Van der Waals had told him.

They were fascinated. "But did you ever meet Raoul Wallenberg?"

Pause.

"No."

"The Swedish Legation was nearby."

"It was across from the family house on Kelenhegyi Street and the Finnish Legation was next door. Wallenberg was hiding thirty Jewish men, women, and children there. He came to the house to find me once, but I was already gone."

"Did he come back?"

"No. I was already in prison in the Soviet Union when he was looking for me. And they took him there later, too. At the time he came to the house, your grandparents were there to open the door. He then met and spoke with the partisan organizer whom my group was hiding."

"Partisan organizer?"

"He was technically a British agent." He shrugged his

shoulders. "Your grandmother told me when I got out of the prison that the partisan organizer met with Raoul Wallenberg when he came to the house looking for me and I was already in prison. It was early 1945. The partisan organizer had been sprung from prison by our group. We bribed the guards. But later, when many had already been arrested, he left. He apparently had no problems with the Russians."

"Was that the only time Raoul Wallenberg came to the house?"

"There were other times before then - when I was still free - because of ALBERT." He went on to recount how he had been helping his good friend in Hungary, who had become an agent of the British Secret Intelligence Service, after which time he was known as ALBERT. And from the way he said ALBERT, one had the sense that he had been someone of importance.

ALBERT was Gabor Haraszty. At that time, he had been leading the group. "We knew a lot of people," Karoly added quietly. "I knew Hannah Senesh."

They waited for him to continue.

"ALBERT reported to Jacques Dubreuil, of ISLD."
He then gave Jack's real name and second alias, but said nothing more of him.

"And the partisan organizer?"

"Daniels. He was just there, hiding at the house."

"Did he know ALBERT?"

"Of course. The servants had instructions that anytime ALBERT came to my apartment, with its separate entrance, they should let him in, even if I was not present. There were underground meetings at my private upstairs apartment and sometimes Raoul Wallenberg was there."

"But you said you didn't know Wallenberg."

"I didn't. He just attended some of the meetings."

"But you must have seen him if you knew he was there."

"No," he said somberly. He then picked up his menu and changed the subject.

They tried to continue with the subject of ALBERT, Raoul Wallenberg, and the mysterious meetings, but to no avail. One had the impression he felt he had already said too much.

Remembering

The Europeans who had attended Karoly Schandl's funeral were now gathered in the spacious front entrance of the funeral home. It seemed only fitting that the décor was the same understated elegance as the places he and his friends would have frequented in Hungary, prior to the Second World War.

Friends and relatives gathered to remember him.

But his children were quietly out of place. Due to circumstance, their culture was the culture of the Cold War.

The typical demeanor of some men and women from the old era was entirely foreign to them, for neither Karoly nor his wife had ever been pretentious. Karoly had been more preoccupied with justice. That was the lawyer in him. In Hungary, he had obtained his doctorate in Law (becoming a qualified lawyer and judge), as well as the designation of a Chartered Accountant. He was a firm believer in facts, details, and playing by the rules.

Perhaps his endless quest for truth and justice had led him to share with one of his grown-up children some additional writings he'd completed earlier. It was no coincidence that it was the same offspring who had attempted, without success, to further probe into his mysterious past.

"I would like you to help me edit something," he'd announced one day, a twinkle in his eye.

"Are you writing a book about the Russian prisons?" People had always told him he should.

"No. I already wrote something about the Yagoda siren and some other matters a long time ago. This is different. And when you are finished reading it, you can tell me what you think."

It was a manuscript of sorts, and the first noticeable thing was the fact that the name of the main character was not his name.

"It contains part of what happened."

"I thought it was a story."

"Parts of it are real," he said cryptically...

And so parts of it were real. The story described the case of the young accountant who had helped a noble cause and was then arrested for his efforts. The Soviet authorities had accused him of having had contact with an anti-Soviet organization for the purpose of spying. The young man had gathered information, it was true, but he had not been spying. He had been helping a cause. The Soviets hadn't seen it that way, however. They had accused him of working for a "big American spy" and also sometimes meeting with an important Colonel (neither of whom was mentioned by name).

The NKVD were also angry at the fact that the young accountant and his friend had been working with "chickens."

Some of the writings had been written in MI9 code.

Interestingly, Gabor Haraszty had gone to Yugoslavia and Bari in May 1944, so as to coordinate the group's activities with Chicken Operations, which were Jewish rescue operations. ALBERT, Karoly, and the group were going to work with Chicken Operations and they would have succeeded - had the Hungarian counter-intelligence in Nazi-occupied Hungary not arrested some of the key players in Chicken Operations, including Hannah Senesh, Perez Goldstein, and Joel Palgi.

The Soviets, it seemed, had been very nervous about the past and intended contacts of Gabor Haraszty's group.

Perhaps that was why they had escorted Schandl and Van der Waals to Moscow by plane from Bucharest, under heavily armed guard in January 1945 – along with members of the Abwehr, German military intelligence.

THE VISITOR

At Karoly Schandl's funeral, there was a man Karoly's wife and adult children did not recognize. He was short and stocky, with a mass of dark hair which looked as though it could have been a wig.

He had not been invited to the funeral by the family, yet he had somehow heard about it and decided to show up. He approached the immediate family members without telling them who he was and how he had known Karoly - decades earlier.

He was not wearing a suit.

Who exactly had sent him?

The man addressed them in English, which he spoke with a thick accent.

His first question to Karoly's adult children was about the cause of death. "Was he sick? Had he been sick?"

When they replied that he had been ill, he nodded, as if he had known.

"But it was so sudden!"

In fact, it was not sudden. Karoly had been battling an illness for months.

They then realized this man was a stranger - a dishonest one.

The man got straight to the point.

"Did he say or write anything?"

They looked at him blankly

He attempted to elaborate. "Did he ever say anything about the Russians? Anything at all?"

The unknown man's eyes were intense.

They replied they did not know anything.

He persisted with his questions.

"Is there anything you can remember? Did he write anything? Is there anything you can tell me, anything at all?"

The answer was still a polite no.

He then stated he was writing a book.

They did not respond.

When he realized he would not obtain any information, he excused himself, and went on to the next person. Eventually, however, he must have perceived that he had been noticed by one of Karoly Schandl's old school friends from Hungary, who came to stand beside the family and observed him.

The man suddenly sat down, shaking his head and muttering to himself.

"This is not good. Not good."

His anxiety in having been recognized was evident as beads of perspiration formed on his face.

Moments later, he was gone.

That was the only time the descendants of Karoly Schandl ever saw "Daniels," the so-called British agent who had been hiding at the Schandl villa in World War II Hungary.

After he had filed his reports in the U.K. in 1945, Daniels was required to provide more details and names of those with whom he had been in contact in Hungary. Thus, he had to file a supplement to his report – and that was when he finally admitted having been privy to a meeting at Schandl's home. It was the early December 1944 meeting attended by Barratt, Clement, Schandl, and Kari. Daniels admitted he had also been present and had heard Schandl, Clement, and Barratt discussing details of how they would report to the Russians. In the supplement to his report, it was also evident that Daniels was aware that Schandl, Clement, and Barratt all disappeared shortly thereafter - though he would later try to rewrite history by pretending Schandl had never gone missing and that the "Clement" he had met had not even been a British agent ...

And yet 45 years later, Daniels showed up at Karoly Schandl's funeral to find out how much Schandl had told his family.

CHAPTER 27
SURVEILLANCE

Most historians and journalists are interested in facts. In times of war, there are often agents among them, whose function is to collect and selectively spread information. During the Second World War, for example, the British used the services of a well known Hungarian journalist who was paid by them for such a purpose. He became a "propagandist" and an "agent" of the Allies. [1]

During the Cold War, the well oiled Communist propaganda machine took misinformation to a brazen level. Smear campaigns preceded internationally illegal actions and human rights violations. Prior to this death, Joseph Stalin was making preparations for the famous Jewish doctor plot, in which show trials of Jewish doctors accused of plotting to poison him were planned. After the arrests of the doctors had been made, two Russian Jewish doctors were placed in the Special Section of Vladimir prison, where prisoners were secretly held as numbers, so as to conceal their identity. One of the Jewish doctors was placed in the cell across from Karoly Schandl. [2]

His crime - being in contact with an international Zionist organization.

In all, hundreds were accused. Pravda reported that a group of saboteur doctors had been arrested. It was stated that the doctors had been plotting to kill the Soviet leadership through medical sabotage and that they had been recruited by a division of American intelligence who operated under the pretense of a Jewish charity. Following Stalin's sudden death, the entire "plot" was declared a fabrication of Stalin and his circle.

Under the Soviet umbrella, Communist Hungary at times displayed a more underhanded approach to covering up the criminality of the totalitarian state – at least in the later years. Trustworthy party members were sometimes sent abroad, pretending to be journalists who spread the word of how one could now criticize the government. It was an attempt at convincing the outside world (in which there were hundreds of thousands of Hungarians who had escaped) that things in Hungary were not as austere as in the past.

But that did not change the fact that other Hungarians remained imprisoned in the Soviet Union. *The last one to be released was a 75 year old World War II veteran, who finally returned home after fifty-five years of captivity. He was found in a Russian mental hospital and returned in the year 2000, ten years after the Communists had been removed from power in Hungary.*

The journalists sent abroad during the totalitarian era were not exactly as democracy-minded as they wished to present themselves. One was a suspected former NKVD agent who had also been one of the appointed judges in a sham trial involving a high ranking member of the clergy – who had been drugged prior to his trial.

There were also members of the artistic community who were sent abroad, to arrange performances and then present speeches about the great virtues of Marxism. They generally fell on deaf ears and the eager messengers sometimes found themselves explaining the purpose of their visit to the free world to extremely curious authorities who had been tipped off by more than a few in the audience.

After the fall of communism, the era of secrecy and misinformation presumably ended – at least for most...

WHO WAS LIEUTENANT WAALS?
Ki Volt Waals Hadnagy?

It was a seemingly innocent article which appeared in a Hungarian newspaper in 1992, written by a well respected historian/journalist. He had been employed as a historian and journalist during the communist era and seemed to have accomplished a great deal within its restrictions. [3]

His real reasons for writing the article are unknown.

The title was *Who Was Lieutenant Waals?* and in May 1992, it appeared in a nationally circulated Hungarian newspaper. [4]

What was the source? Karoly Schandl had been conveniently deceased for two years. He had passed away in February 1990 – two years earlier. Furthermore, he had never returned to Hungary during his lifetime, nor had he ever spoken to any interviewer about Gerit Van der Waals and Gabor Haraszty.

Unless one considered a Communist interrogation from any period between 1944 and 1956 a legitimate interview.

Thus, the information for the article had been entirely procured from semi-accurate Communist-era files. They must have been semi-accurate, for the article erroneously quoted Schandl's death as 1986 (instead of 1990), and assigned Karoly Schandl and Gerit Van der Waals the same 11 year prison record, although Van der Waals had died after approximately a year of captivity. It was also given an unusual slant - not in favor of Gabor Haraszty. [5]

It stated that in 1944, 12 Dutch officers from the Dutch Underground, including Gerit Van der Waals, made contact with the British Secret Service through Karoly Schandl. [6]

This was inaccurate. As documented in the British National Archives, Gerit Van der Waals sometimes functioned as a cut-out courier, and the British considered him a British agent. He had also been linked to Colonel Howie. Colonel Howie, the highest ranking British Officer, made contact with Van Der Waals via his Polish contacts at Zugliget, the Polish internment camp on the outskirts of Budapest. At Howie's request, Van der Waals introduced him to "Smit," operator of Philips radio in the Balkans. By 1944, Howie was involved in a network of the British Secret Intelligence Service, the Dutch Underground, and the Polish Underground. Howie had contact with Dubreuil, the original leader of Schandl's group, and Gabor Haraszty, who was also in the same group.

Schandl and Gerit Van der Waals met when Van der Waals came to Schandl's home to take photographs and make fake IDs for the two refugees hiding in his home. In addition to his role as a British courier, Van der Waals by then was working for Raoul Wallenberg, producing fake documents to help people escape Nazi persecution. Van der Waals had made hundreds of such IDs. [7]

Although the article did later acknowledge that he had prepared false IDs, no mention was made of the fact that he had done this work for Raoul Wallenberg.

According to the article, the Dutch made contact with the British through Karoly Schandl – at least they thought they did and they thought that at the end of this chain was the central London Office. Van der Waals asked Schandl to help him across the Russian lines and Schandl's friend Gabor Haraszty, who had British connections, advised Schandl to go. ... The password was "We are the friends of Albert." The article claimed that Schandl and Van der Waals had wanted to be forwarded to the Tito partisans, then to Italy. It also implied that Gabor Haraszty had not been a link to the British after all. Schandl and Van der Waals were arrested by the Soviets. [8]

The documented truth was that Gabor Haraszty was a trained and very active agent of the British Intelligence Service (ISLD) who was also connected to MI9 - and had been in contact with Zionists, with whom he and his group had planned to work in Budapest.

Furthermore, as Karoly Schandl stated in his memoirs, he had been instructed to take Van der Waals across the Russian lines – as per a British order. The Russians were to forward Van der Waals to the British Intelligence Service and Schandl to the alleged newly formed anti-Nazi Hungarian government.

Though the article did not accurately report on all of the facts, it did, however, contain one item of interest – namely that after his release, Schandl was known to have contacted Van der Waals' Dutch family to tell them all he knew. [9]

Karoly Schandl would only have been able to do this after he had fled Communist Hungary – and he had never told anyone about it.

It seemed that even after he'd made it to the free world, he had been watched ...

He'd always suspected as much.

Notes:

1. HS 4/129
2. C. Schandl, *Sword of the Turul* (Lulu Press 2005) *see Schandl's memoirs*
3. Macskasy, P. *Ki Volt Waals hadnagy?* (May 7, 1992)
4. Ibid
5. Ibid
6. Ibid
7. C. Schandl, *Sword of the Turul* (Lulu Press 2005)
8. Macskasy, P. *Ki Volt Waals Hadnagy?* (May 7, 1992)

EPILOGUE

"In the 1930s, I was a Boy Scout, and my group of Boy Scouts (the Piarist Boy Scouts) made some friends in Poland, where we attended a Jamboree. One of our Polish friends, "Jack," later fled to Hungary in October 1939. We helped him, sheltered him. He was naturally in contact with the Polish Legation in Hungary, as long as it existed, and remained there as an agent after the Legation left Budapest.

One by one, all unmarried members of our Boy Scout group got involved in the 'illegal activities' of the resistance. We had vowed to help not only our friend Jack and the Poles, but also our Jewish friends and whoever we were able to help.

It was the Boy Scout spirit that survived, even after the dissolution of the Boy Scout organizations. One of my friends in the group, a young (Jewish) Hungarian lawyer, Gabriel (Gabor) Haraszthy, was active in supporting Allied prisoners (English, French, Dutch, etc.) who reached Hungary from German prison camps. He visited Alexandria (Egypt) through the Tito partisans early in 1944 and was dropped in Hungary later from Bari, as an official agent of the British to organize and lead our group. He was then known as 'Albert.'

During the Nazi occupation, our group used to take escaped Allied prisoners-of-war from Hungary to the Tito partisans, with monthly reports to 'the Center.' The partisans had their weekly supply planes arriving from Alexandria or Bari, and the escaped prisoners were the load to be taken back.

On the request of 'Albert,' who was then an Officer of the British Intelligence Service, I was asked to accompany Dutch Lieutenant Gerit Van der Waals over the fighting lines to the Soviet troops in December 1944. The Russians were supposed to forward the Dutch Lieutenant to the I.S. (British Intelligence Service), and myself to the allegedly formed new anti-Nazi Hungarian government ...

I left a partisan organizer, who was freed from prison camp by the group, and a Jewish school friend with my parents, and departed from Budapest with the Dutchman to reach the Russian troops ...

'Albert' told me that he himself would go to the Russian commander on the arrival of the Russians in Budapest, in his British uniform, to ask for transportation and food for the escapees in hiding - and so he did, but he did not survive the treatment he received from the Russian NKVD ..."

*Karoly Schandl, 1961
(partial memoirs in 'Sword of the Turul')*

In early 1944, Gabor Haraszty became a trained agent of the Secret Intelligence Service and was then known as ALBERT. [1]

His group had links to Colonel Howie, the Dutch Underground, the Tito partisans, the Polish Underground, and Jewish parachutists from Palestine.

Lajos - Louis - Tibor Clement (Klement) visited Karoly Schandl's home and also worked with the group.[2] Clement was an agent of the Special Operations Executive who had been sent into Hungary by being dropped into Poland.[3] Clement was also the radio operator who transmitted intelligence for Dubreuil and Lafayette of the British Intelligence Service, as well as Colonel Howie, and Van Hootegem.[4]

Dubreuil was an alias of the Polish ISLD agent who started the intelligence network of Piarist Boy Scouts for resistance purposes. His old Boy Scout friends in that network included Karoly Schandl and Gabor Haraszty. They had known each other since childhood, and first met Dubreuil at a 1932 Boy Scouts Jamboree in Poland. [5]

"The group" included not only Karoly Schandl and Gabor Haraszty, but also other Piarist Boy Scouts alumni. It was a network of friends. Other Piarist friends who were involved with the group were Peter Zerkowitz and Raphael Rupert. Peter Zerkowitz sometimes used the radio Gabor Haraszty had hidden in his family villa in Buda.

Shortly after the war, the British Military Mission were advised that if necessary, they could contact Raphael Rupert through Peter Zerkowitz.[6]

Gabor Haraszty, Karoly Schandl, Peter Zerkowitz, and Raphael Rupert had all been friends. Clement and Barratt had been working with them.

Both Schandl and Zerkowitz reported knowing Dubreuil, a.k.a. "Jack," the Polish friend who played a key role in British intelligence (ISLD) in Hungary, though Rupert never referred to him by name.

Rupert - who helped Reginald Barratt - did, however, admit he had been involved in a "British" group which gathered intelligence in Budapest.[7] Rupert had been a Piarist alumni, so it is quite evident that he would have known "Jack" as well.

Gabor Haraszty's group of helpers and friends – which was in turn led by Dubreuil of the ISLD – was liquidated by the Soviets.

Rupert was carted off to a gulag in 1946.[8]

Peter Zerkowitz narrowly escaped the Communist Secret Police in 1946. His brother was less fortunate and perished in a gulag. *Karoly Schandl gave Peter the sad news in the U.S., fifteen years later.*

Gabor Haraszty and Reginald Barratt were said to have been killed by the Soviets shortly after the siege of Budapest.

Barratt was arrested by the Soviets and reportedly shot.[9]

Gabor Haraszty was also reportedly shot by the Russians.

Schandl and Van der Waals were arrested by the NKVD in Hungary.

Schandl, Clement, Van der Waals, and Pap were taken to the Soviet Union, where they were imprisoned.

Van der Waals perished in Lefortovo prison.

In 1950, Karoly Schandl was moved to the Special Section of Vladimir prison.

He was not released by the Communists until 1956.

From 1991 to 2001, at the request of Raoul Wallenberg's brother, a Swedish-Russian joint Commission was set up to investigate the fate of Swedish Diplomat Raoul Wallenberg. The commission discovered that 3 Hungarian numbered prisoners secretly held in isolation in Vladimir prison had been connected to the Wallenberg case

They were Schandl, Pap, and Clement.[10]

As Karoly Schandl stated in his memoirs (see excerpt in *Sword of the Turul, 2005*), both Schandl and Laszlo Pap had been helping Gabor Haraszty in Budapest. [11] Clement was also working with the group and visited Schandl's home on more than one occasion. [12]

All three numbered prisoners had been working together in World War II Budapest, in the British-led anti-Nazi resistance group of Gabor Haraszty, and thus the ISLD network of Jacques Dubreuil.

Karoly had known both Gabor Haraszty and "Jacques Dubreuil" for years, well before they were drawn into the intelligence game of the British underground. [13]

Karoly William Schandl was my father

Gabor Haraszty - a.k.a. British agent ALBERT - was his best friend.

Catherine Eva Schandl, M.Ed.

Notes:

1. C. Schandl, *Sword of the Turul* (Lulu Press 2005)
2. i. HS 9/461/7
   ii. HS 4/246
3. W. Mackenzie, *The Secret History of S.O.E.* (St. Ermin's Press 2000, 2002)
4. HS 4/103
5. C. Schandl, *Sword of the Turul* (Lulu Press 2005)
6. HS 4/129
7. Raphael Rupert, *Red Wire and the Lubianka* (Ballinakella 1991)
8. Ibid
9. Ibid
10. Marvin W. Makinen and Ari D. Kaplan, *Cell Occupancy Analysis of Korpus 2 of the Vladimir Prison* (Report Submitted to the Swedish-Russian Working Group on the Fate of Raoul Wallenberg December 15, 2000)
    See prisoners "Schandel," "Pap," "Klement"
11. C. Schandl, *Sword of the Turul* (Lulu Press 2005)
12. i. HS 9/461/7
    ii. HS 4/246
13. C. Schandl, *Sword of the Turul* (Lulu Press 2005)
    see Schandl's memoirs

This is an official document from the Hungarian Defense Department Archives. It shows that the date of Karoly Schandl's official arrest as a "prisoner-of-war" by the Red Army was on **December 8, 1944** and that his imprisonment in the Soviet Union was for 11 years *(from 1950 on, he was held as a "British spy")*.

MAGYAR HONVÉDSÉG
KÖZPONTI IRATTÁR
Nyt. szám: 331/1323/11/Kné

1. számú példány

1994 -08- 31

Canada

Tárgy: Hadifogsági idő
igazolása

A fenti parancsnokság birtokában levő iratok szerint: néhai Dr. Schandl Károly (1912. Menyhárt Teréz) mint főhadnagy

1944.12.08. - 1950.08.01-ig hadifogolyként,
1950.08.02. - 1956.05.18-ig elítéltként tartózkodott a Szovjetunióban.

Budapest, 1994. augusztus 25 -n

A távollévő parancsnok helyett:

/Bíró Géza őrnagy/
parancsnokhelyettes

Készült: 2 példányban
Egy példány: 1 lap
Itsz.: 2104

eMediaWire
PRWeb NEWSWIRE

March 11, 2006

Author Reveals Names of Betrayed Hungarian Heroes

What really happened to the British led anti-Nazi resistance in World War II Hungary - and who they were.

Toronto, CA (PRWEB) March 11, 2006 -- "Sword of the Turul," by Catherine Eva Schandl, tells the true story of how the British-led anti-Nazi resistance in Hungary was secretly imprisoned by the NKVD and abandoned by the British intelligence service after World War II. The only thing missing from the book is names. The author is now disclosing the real names of: the Hungarian leader of her father Karoly's resistance group, one of the group members who also ended up in Vladimir prison, and the arrested Dutch lieutenant who was working for Raoul Wallenberg.

"I am revealing these names because Hungary's National Day of March 15 (war of independence) is approaching," the author explains, "and Hungarians have a right to know about all their heroes and what really happened to them."

Karoly William Schandl, a Hungarian lawyer, was a survivor of almost 12 years in the Soviet prisons of Lubyanka, Lefortovo, and Vladimir. Prior to his official arrest by the NKVD/SMERSH on December 8, 1944, he was a member of a British led anti-Nazi resistance group, and lived across from Raoul Wallenberg's Swedish Embassy in Budapest. In early December 1944 - south of Lake Velence - SMERSH arrested Karoly Schandl, along with a Dutch lieutenant who had been working for Swedish diplomat Raoul Wallenberg. British intelligence had ordered them to report to the Russians.

The Dutch lieutenant was G. Van der Waals.

Karoly and Lt. Van der Waals were placed in Lubyanka and then Lefortovo prison.

The leader of Karoly's group, Gabor Haraszty (code name "Albert"), was a young Hungarian lawyer of Jewish origin who had become an officer of the British Intelligence Service. He too was later arrested by SMERSH. He did not survive.

After 5 years as a POW, Karoly was accused of being a "British spy." In 1950, he was transferred to Vladimir prison, where he was kept locked away in secret, in the "special section," near another friend from his resistance group, Laszlo Pap, who had also been arrested. The Soviets continued to deny any knowledge of their whereabouts.

(Lt. Van der Waals had already perished years earlier in Lefortovo prison)

Karoly Schandl was finally released by the Soviets in 1956. Shortly afterwards, he went to Whitehall (U.K.) and told them that members of the British-led resistance were still secretly imprisoned in the Soviet Union. Whitehall, however, was not willing to listen.

To date, MI6 has not offered any explanation.

(Russia has since opened up a number of files and released Karoly Schandl's secret prison card to the joint Swedish-Russian Wallenberg Commission in 1990, as one of only three Hungarians secretly held in Vladimir prison, assigned a number)

More information about this true story can be found at:

www.swordoftheturul.com

BIBLIOGRAPHY

Susanne Berger, *Stuck in Neutral: The Reasons behind Sweden's Passivity in the Raoul Wallenberg case* (August 2005)

John Bierman, *The Secret Life of Laszlo Almasy: The Real English Patient* (Penguin Books 2004)

Eichmann Trial Transcripts (Nizkor Project)

M.R.D. Foot & J.M. Langley, *MI9 Escape and Evasion 1939-1945* (Bodley Head 1979)

F.S. Jones, *The Double Dutchman* (Corgi Books 1978)

K. Kapronczay *Refugees in Hungary: Shelter from the Storm During World War II* (Matthias Corvinus Publishing 1999)

Stephen Kertesz, *Between Russia and the West* (University of Notre Dame Press 1984)

Henry Kissinger, *Diplomacy* (Simon and Schuster 1994)

W. Mackenzie, *The Secret History of S.O.E.* (St. Ermin's Press 2000, 2002)

Marvin W. Makinen and Ari D. Kaplan, *Cell Occupancy Analysis of Korpus 2 of the Vladimir Prison* (Report Submitted to the Swedish-Russian Working Group on the Fate of Raoul Wallenberg, December 15, 2000)

Michael Ondaatje, *The English Patient* (Vintage 1993)

Y. Palgi, *Into the Inferno: the Memoir of a Jewish Paratrooper Behind Nazi Lines* (Rutgers University Press 2003)

Raphael Rupert, *Red Wire and the Lubianka* (Ballinakella 1991)

C. Schandl, *Sword of the Turul* (Lulu Press 2005)

H. Senesh, *Hannah Senesh: Her Life and Diary, the First complete Edition* (Jewish Lights Publishing 2004)

A. Simon, Miklos Horthy, *Annotated Memoirs of Admiral Miklos Horthy, The Regent of Hungary* (1996)

Istvan Szent-Miklosy, *With the Hungarian Independence Movement 1943-1947* (Praeger Publishers 1988)

Krisztian Ungvary, *The Siege of Budapest: 100 Days in World War II* (I.B. Taurus 2002, Yale University Press 2005)

Raoul Wallenberg, *Letters and Dispatches 1924-1944* (Arcade Publishing 1996)

Alex Weissberg, *Desperate Mission: Joel Brand's Story* (Criterion Books 1958)

L.P. Wilkinson, *Kingsmen of a Century 1873-1972* (King's College, Cambridge University Press 1980, 1981)

The Memoirs and other private writings of Karoly Schandl

Various PRO documents, U.K. National Archives (The Crown retains copyright).

ABOUT THE AUTHOR

Catherine Eva Schandl, B.A. Honours, M.Ed., is a Canadian-born writer, researcher, and university instructor of Hungarian origin. She completed a B.A. Honours in French Studies at York University and obtained a Master of English Language Education from the University of Tasmania. She is also a black belt in martial arts.

Catherine is the author of the well received book *Sword of the Turul*, which has been mentioned on the website of the International Raoul Wallenberg Foundation, due to its historical merit. The book can also be found in Yad Vashem library.

The London-Budapest Game is the sequel to *Sword of the Turul,* offering a unique glimpse into the dangerous game of the British underground in Hungary – and its aftermath.

See also

www.swordoftheturul.com

www.karolyschandl.com

www.catherineschandl.com

INDEX OF NAMES

ALBERT (see Haraszty Gabor)
Almasy, Laszlo   p. 132, 133, 134

Barratt, Reginald   p. 31, 38, 72, 83, 86, 89, 91, 92, 95, 97, 98, 99, 101, 116, 122, 123, 125, 130, 166, 184, 193

Berdichev, Sgt.   p. 43, 47
Bethlen, Count Istvan   p. 15, 70, 71, 74, 75, 177
Bowlby, Col. ISLD   p. 50
Brackel, Frank   p. 97, 98
Brand, Joel   p. 24, 25, 33, 34, 55, 57, 58, 59, 60, 82, 122
Churchill, Winston   p. 28, 43, 45, 68, 75

Clement, Lajos/Louis/Tibor   p. 20, 21, 32, 33, 38, 39, 81, 83, 84, 89, 91, 100, 101, 116, 117, 118, 119, 120, 123, 124, 125, 149, 163, 184, 192, 193, 194

Csuros, L.   p.116
Dafni, Reuven (Gary)   p. 43, 44, 45, 47, 49, 50, 60, 70, 92

Daniels, Lt.   p. 81, 82, 83, 84, 89, 107, 108, 110 119, 124, 125, 180, 183, 184

Dubreuil, Jacques ("Jack")   p. 29, 30, 32, 81, 82, 99, 100, 116, 125, 132, 167, 168, 180, 188, 191, 192, 193, 194

Eichmann, Adolf   p. 26, 33, 34, 57, 58, 60, 72
Foot, M.R.D.   p. 40
Garzuly (Garcoly), Colonel   p. 82, 83
Gary (see Reuven Dafni)
Goldstein, Perez   p. 43, 45, 46, 50, 51, 55, 56, 57, 58, 59, 61, 80, 81, 82, 128, 182

Haraszty, Gabor   p. 6, 13, 14, 29, 30, 31, 32, 33, 34, 38, 39, 42, 43, 44, 45, 46, 47, 48, 49, 50, 51, 68, 69, 74, 79, 80, 81, 88, 90, 91, 92, 93, 99, 116, 122, 123, 124, 129, 147, 148, 155, 165, 168, 174, 180, 182,

              187, 188, 189, 191, 192, 193, 194, 197

Haraszty, Karoly   p. 28, 155, 165, 174
Horthy, Regent   p. 70, 71, 72, 73, 74, 75, 76, 77
Horthy, Nicholas Jr. p. 75-77

Howie, Colonel   p.6, 22, 23, 24, 25, 26, 32, 42, 43, 46, 47, 70, 71,
                       72, 73, 74, 90, 97, 98, 99, 100, 101, 114, 115,
                       122, 188, 192

Jones (see Perez Goldstein)
Kallay, Miklos   p. 26, 28, 29, 31, 43, 45
Kasztner, Rudolf   p. 55, 57, 58, 59, 82, 94
Klement (see Clement)
Komoly, Otto   p. 82, 122
Lafayette   p. 32, 100, 192
Langley, J.M.   p. 40
Lawson   p. 46, 47, 48, 92
'Leopold'   p. 163
Micky (see Joel Palgi)
Minnie (see Hannah Senesh)
Natusch, Roy   p. 23, 24, 42, 70, 72, 97, 98, 99, 100, 101
Nussbacher (see Joel Palgi)

Palgi, Joel   p. 43, 45, 51, 54, 55, 56, 57, 58, 59, 60, 61, 62,
                   80, 81, 82, 83, 84, 86, 87, 91, 92, 93, 105,
                   106, 128, 129, 130, 131, 162, 182

Pap, Laszlo   p. 147, 149, 194, 195, 198
Puckel, William   p. 124
Rupert, Raphael   p. 31, 80, 86, 87, 123, 124, 162, 193
Salkahazi,Sara   p.144
Schandl, Joseph   p. 3, 166
(Jozsef)

Schandl, Karoly (Charles)
chapters 1, 2, 5, 6, 9, 11, 13, 14, 15, 16, 19, 20, 21, 22, 23, 24, 25, 26, 27, epilogue

Schandl, Karoly (Senior) p. 15, 16, 17, 65, 80, 107, 108, 109, 110,
                           154, 166, 177

Schandl, Terezia p. 15, 16, 65, 66, 108, 144, 155, 177

Senesh, Hannah   p. 43, 44, 45, 46, 47, 51, 56, 60, 61, 80, 81, 82, 85, 87, 128, 180, 182

Simonds, A.C.   p. 40, 46, 49, 50, 128
Smit p. 23, 90, 164, 188
Szladits, Karoly (Charles) p. 31, 48, 80, 86, 92
Stalin, Joseph p. 72, 75, 84, 106, 151, 185, 186
Szalasi, Ferenc p.76, 79
Szent-Gyorgyi p.28
Szent-Ivanyi, Reverend p. 23, 24, 42, 98, 114
Szent-Miklosy, Istvan p. 30, 31, 79
Taylor, R.S. p. 49
Tasker, Gordon p.101

Van der Waals, Gerit p. 23, 89, 90, 91, 93, 94, 95, 103, 113, 122, 123, 124, 136, 144, 145, 157, 163, 164, 179, 182, 187, 188, 189, 191, 193, 194, 197, 198

Van Hootegem, Edward p.32, 97, 98, 99, 100, 101, 102, 192
Veres, Mr. (father of Thomas Veres) p.16, 17
Veres, Laszlo p.28, 29
Voroshilov   p.117, 119
Wallenberg, Raoul p. 6, 16, 64, 65, 67, 69, 73, 90, 95, 123, 133, 144, 145, 153, 157, 158, 178, 179, 180, 181, 188, 194, 197, 198

Weinstein   p. 22, 24, 98, 99, 122, 123, 124
Zerkowitz, Peter p. 30, 31, 68, 79, 163, 166, 193

Printed in Great Britain
by Amazon.co.uk, Ltd.,
Marston Gate.